FROM THE GARDEN

America's
HOME COOKING

Illustration by Jan McEvoy

WQED
PITTSBURGH

WQED
PITTSBURGH

For other great merchandise,
visit ShopWQED.org or call 1/800-274-1307.
Shop WQED, 4802 Fifth Avenue, Pittsburgh, PA 15213

For WQED Multimedia:

President and Chief Executive Officer
Deborah L. Acklin

Director of Distribution
Robyn Martin

Distribution Administrator
Hollie Hepler

America's Home Cooking Producer/Host
Chris Fennimore

Graphic Designer
Audrey Galata

Cookbook Editor
Joyce Carr

Table of Contents

ON-AIR RECIPES

Asparagus with Lemon Garlic
Aioli. 9

Corn and Red Pepper Fritters 10

Creamy Basil Roasted Garlic Tomato
Soup. 11

Garden Tomato Tart 12

Pesto 13

Raspberry Balsamic Vinaigrette. . . . 14

Rhubarb Oatmeal Crisp Dessert 15

Spectacular Butternut Squash
Ravioli. 16

Zucchini Casserole. 17

TOMATOES

Baked Green Tomatoes 21

Baked Whole Tomatoes 22

Breaded Tomatoes with Cheese
Sauce. 23

Bruchetti. 24

Carolyn's Country Garden Quiche 25

Crunchy Fried Tomatoes. 26

Easy Pan Fried Tomatoes. 27

Fire and Ice Tomatoes 28

Fried Green Tomatoes 29

Jan's Good Tomato Recipe. 30

Mediterranean Tomato Salad 31

Plum Tomato Tart 32

Salsa 33

Scalloped Tomatoes 34

Stewed Tomatoes 35

Tomato and Cheese Strata 36

Tomato Fans. 37

Tomato Pie. .38

Tomatoes Oregonata. 39

Yellow Tomato Coulis 40

ZUCCHINI

Grilled Zucchini with Feta. 43

Mock Crab Cakes. 44

Stuffed Zucchini Boats 45

Zucchini Cheesecake. 46

Zucchini Flowers with Goat Cheese and
Mint. 47

Zucchini Fritters 48

Zucchini Pancakes. 49

Zucchini Parmesan. 50

*Recipes were prepared on "America's Home Cooking:
From the Garden"*

Table of Contents

Zucchini Quiche 51

Zucchini Stuffing Casserole 52

MIXED VEGETABLES

Asparagus and Red Pepper
Sauté 55

Broccoli Stir Fry 56

Corn and Basil Egg Roulade 57

Corn and Rock Shrimp Pot Pie 58

Cornmeal Biscuit Dough. 59

Gazpacho I. 60

Glazed Carrots 61

Haricots Verts in Walnut Oil 62

Mediterranean Fish with Fennel and
Kalamata Olives 63

Mixed Vegetables 64

Old Stone Inn Corn Fritters 65

Pesto Chicken 66

Roasted Ratatouille 67

Skillet Vegetables 68

Stuffed Fried Cubanella Sweet
Peppers 69

Succotash. 70

Swiss Chard, Beans and
Tomatoes 71

EGGPLANT

Crepes 75

Eggplant Pizza 76

Eggplant Pudding. 77

Fesenjan-e Bademjan 78

Ratatouille. 79

Ratatouille Crepes 80

Summer Ratatouille 81

PASTA

Bacon-Tomato Angel Hair. 85

Garden Gravy. 86

Handmade Cavatelli. 87

Marinara Sauce 88

Spaghetti with Summer Herbs 89

Sweet Harmony 90

Tomato-Zucchini Stir Fry 91

SALADS AND DRESSING

Broccoli-Tomato Salad 95

Cucumber-Tomato Yogurt. 96

Fresh Tomato Salad 97

Recipes were prepared on "America's Home Cooking: From the Garden"

Table of Contents

Harvest Vegetable Salad 98

Italian Tomato, Mozzarella and Basil
Salad 99

Lamb, Cucumber and Tomato
Salad 100

Make Ahead Salad 101

Pomegranate Carrot Salad 102

Raw Cauliflower and Gorgonzola
Cheese Salad 103

Summertime Picnic Relish 104

Tomato Toast Salad 105

Tomato Vinaigrette 106

Tomatoes and Cucumbers in Sour
Cream 107

Tropical Mango Avocado Salad 108

SOUPS AND STEWS

Celeriac Vichyssoise 111

Fall Clean-Up 112

Fresh Tomato Soup 113

Gazpacho II 114

Greens, Potato and Sausage
Soup 115

Mom's Seven Up 116

Old-Fashioned Tomato Soup 117

Poached Garden Eggs 118

Polish Tomato Soup 119

Sassy Potato Corn Chowder 120

Slew 121

Spring Root Stew 122

Strawberry Soup with Pound Cake
Croutons 123

CANNING AND PRESERVING

24-Hour Zucchini Pickles 127

Gourmet Bar-B-Q Sauce 128

Grandma's Green Tomato
Mincemeat 129

Green Tomato Relish 130

Peperoni All'Agrodolce 131

Piccalilli 132

Pomodori Secchi 133

Spicy Quick Dill Pickles 134

Tomato Butter 135

Tomato Jelly 136

Zucchini Stew 137

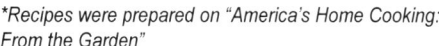

*Recipes were prepared on "America's Home Cooking:
From the Garden"*

Table of Contents

DESSERT

Butternut Squash Bake 141

Butternut Squash Brown Sugar
Pie 142

Chocolate Zucchini Cake 143

Fresh Strawberry Glazed Pie 144

Mock Apple Pie. 145

Pineapple-Rhubarb Pie 146

Spiced Berry Compote 147

INDEX. 149

*Recipes were prepared on "America's Home Cooking:
From the Garden"*

FROM THE GARDEN

America's
HOME COOKING
ON-AIR RECIPES

Asparagus with Lemon Garlic Aioli

DIRECTIONS

To make aioli, add mayonnaise, garlic, lemon juice and lemon zest to a blender, and blend until smooth. Season mixture with salt and pepper, to taste. Chill.

To cook asparagus, rub asparagus with oil, salt and pepper. Over an open flame on medium heat, grill asparagus for seven to ten minutes or until done. Remove asparagus to a platter and drizzle with aioli. Garnish with Roma tomatoes, parmesan cheese and parsley.

INGREDIENTS

1 1/2 cups neutral mayonnaise

6 cloves garlic

1/4 cup fresh lemon juice

2 teaspoons lemon zest

Sea salt and black pepper, to taste

1 bunch asparagus, trimmed

Olive oil

Roma tomatoes, for garnishing

Freshly shaved parmesan cheese, for garnishing

1/4 cup chopped flat leaf parsley, for garnishing

SUBMITTED BY:
Chef Steven Hughes

Corn and Red Pepper Fritters

DIRECTIONS

Mix flour, baking powder, salt and sugar together in a large bowl. Gently stir in egg, milk and melted butter. Use a potato masher to crush about 1/3 of corn kernels. Fold mashed kernels into batter along with the remaining whole kernels and diced pepper. Heat oil and spoon mixture by heaping tablespoon into hot oil. Cook for 2 minutes and turn to cook reverse side until golden brown. Drain on paper towels and top with a little sprinkle of salt.

INGREDIENTS

1 cup sifted all-purpose flour

1 teaspoon baking powder

1/2 teaspoon salt

1/4 teaspoon white sugar

1 egg, lightly beaten

1/2 cup milk

1 tablespoon melted butter

4 ears corn, with kernels sliced off

1 red pepper, finely diced

Oil, for frying

Salt, for garnishing

America's
HOME COOKING

SUBMITTED BY:
Chris Fennimore, WQED Pittsburgh

Creamy Basil Roasted Garlic Tomato Soup

DIRECTIONS

Roast garlic heads. (If a garlic roaster is available, use it to bake garlic heads. If there is no roaster, put garlic in a baking pan or aluminum foil.) Preheat oven to 400 degrees and place garlic heads in baking pan or roaster and drizzle with olive oil. Cook for 30 to 45 minutes, until brown. Remove heads and let cool. Peel garlic and set soft garlic aside.

Core tomatoes and blanch by dipping into a pan of boiling water for 15 seconds and letting them cool. The skins will slip off easily. Cut tomatoes in half and remove seeds. They can be diced at this point, but if a smoother texture is desired, cut tomatoes into quarters and cook for 5 minutes in a saucepan with some olive oil; put them into a food processor.

In a medium saucepan, heat olive oil and cook minced garlic for 1 minute. Add tomatoes and sea salt and cook sauce down for about 10 minutes, or until the consistency is right. (If you want it thinner, add a little chicken stock; thicker, keep cooking.)

Add roasted garlic and heavy cream. Season with salt and pepper to taste. Turn off heat and add basil. (It will wilt in soup but retain its wonderful flavor.)

INGREDIENTS

2 heads roasted garlic, mashed

5 medium tomatoes, blanched, peeled and diced

Olive oil

5 cloves garlic, minced

Sea salt, to taste

1 cup heavy cream

Freshly ground pepper, to taste

1 cup basil chiffonade

SUBMITTED BY:
Doug Oster, from his book
"Tomatoes Garlic Basil" (St. Lynn's Press)

Garden Tomato Tart

DIRECTIONS

Preheat oven to 450 degrees. In a food processor, combine garlic, oregano, basil and 1 tablespoon olive oil to form a paste. Line a 10-inch tart pan (with removable bottom) with pie crust, pressing crust into corners. Trim dough flush with edges and refrigerate for 30 minutes.

Spread garlic mixture on chilled crust. Sprinkle with half of the grated cheese. Arrange tomato slices on top of cheese, overlapping in a circular pattern. Season with salt and pepper, to taste. Sprinkle with remaining cheese and drizzle with remaining 2 tablespoons olive oil. Place in oven and reduce temperature to 400 degrees. Bake until crust is golden and tomatoes are soft, but still retain their shape, about 45 to 55 minutes. Transfer to a wire rack and cool for 20 minutes. Serve warm.

INGREDIENTS

2 to 3 cloves garlic

Fresh oregano and basil, to taste

3 tablespoons olive oil

1 (12-inch) single pie crust

2 ounces fontina cheese, grated (about 1/2 cup)

1 1/2 pounds firm, ripe tomatoes, cored and sliced 1/4 inch thick

Salt and freshly ground black pepper

America's
HOME COOKING

SUBMITTED BY:
Ruth E. Platek, Robinson Township

Pesto

DIRECTIONS

Carefully wash and dry basil and parsley (use a salad spinner if available). In a food processor with metal blade attached, process basil and parsley; add garlic, nuts and cheese. With processor running, drizzle in olive oil. Add salt and pepper, to taste. Put mixture in a jar and cover with a thin layer of olive oil.

INGREDIENTS

2 cups tightly packed basil leaves

1/2 cup fresh parsley

2 cloves garlic

1/2 cup pignoli nuts

1/2 cup romano cheese

1/2 cup olive oil

Salt and pepper

Raspberry Balsamic Vinaigrette

DIRECTIONS

Put all ingredients in a blender or food processor or use an immersion blender to emulsify. Serve as a dressing for salads or a dip for crudités.

INGREDIENTS

1 pint fresh raspberries

1/4 cup balsamic vinegar

3/4 cup extra virgin olive oil

Salt and fresh black pepper, to taste

America's
HOME COOKING

SUBMITTED BY:
Chris Fennimore, WQED Pittsburgh

Rhubarb Oatmeal Crisp Dessert

Directions

Melt butter in a sauce pan and add cornstarch and sugar. Stir until blended; add rhubarb. Over medium heat, cook mixture until rhubarb is soft, about 6 minutes, stirring gently. Remove from heat and cool. When rhubarb mixture is cool, spread into a greased 9-inch square baking pan.

Preheat oven to 375 degrees. To make topping, m x together the first 6 topping ingredients. M x cold butter cubes into flour mixture until it resembles coarse crumbs. Sprinkle over filling in baking pan. Bake for 35 to 40 minutes. Serve with whipped cream or ice cream, if desired. Serves 6 to 8.

Note

This recipe is sent in loving memory of my parents, Helen (1918-2004) and Edwin Betz (1909-2008), lifelong Pittsburgh residents who found all sorts of creative uses for rhubarb from their garden that they shared with many. This recipe is fun and easy and with fresh rhubarb from the garden—the rest of the ingredients are in the kitchen cupboard. It is usually eaten before it gets cold.

Ingredients

3 tablespoons butter

1 tablespoon cornstarch

1/2 cup sugar

1 pound fresh rhubarb, cut into 1/2-inch pieces

Topping:

3/4 cup packed brown sugar

3/4 cup all-purpose flour

3/4 cup old fashioned oats

1/2 teaspoon ground cinnamon

1/4 teaspoon nutmeg

1/4 teaspoon salt

1/2 cup cold butter, cut into cubes

Submitted by:
Mary Ellen Meyer, Pittsburgh

Spectacular Butternut Squash Ravioli

DIRECTIONS

Preheat oven to 400 degrees. Peel butternut squash and remove seeds. Cut into medium-size cubes. Place on a sheet pan and toss with olive oil and salt. Roast for 25 to 30 minutes, tossing once, until very tender. (Squash should reach a caramelized color as well.) While still hot, run squash through ricer to mash. Fold in ricotta cheese, an additional sprinkling of salt, egg yolk, parsley and cheese.

Double up wontons and place 1 to 1 1/2 teaspoons of filling on it and fold in half, forming a triangle. Seal wonton using egg white beaten with a few drops of water. Place each completed ravioli on a wax paper-lined cookie sheet until ready to cook. When ready to cook, lift wax paper and dunk into boiling water. Raviolis will loosen from the wax paper on their own. Boil for about 3 minutes or until tender. Do not dump pasta to strain; using a spider or metal basket, lift pasta from boiling water and drain. Serve with a favorite pasta sauce.

INGREDIENTS

1 (2-pound) butternut squash

2 tablespoons olive oil

Kosher salt, to taste

1 (15-ounce) container ricotta cheese

1 egg yolk and white, separated

2 teaspoons fresh or frozen parsley

1/4 cup freshly grated parmesan cheese

2 (14-ounce) packages wonton wrappers

America's
HOME COOKING

SUBMITTED BY:
Alice Sande

Zucchini Casserole

Directions

Preheat oven to 350 degrees. Sauté chopped meat and onion in a large pan over medium heat until meat is browned and onion is tender. Season with fennel, salt and pepper. Butter the bottom and sides of a 9x13-inch casserole. Cover bottom with bread cubes and lay down a layer of zucchini slices. Pour meat and onion mixture over top and sprinkle with shredded mozzarella and 1/4 cup romano cheese. Top with another layer of zucchini slices and a layer of bread cubes. Dot top with butter and sprinkle with remaining romano cheese. Cover with aluminum foil and bake for 40 minutes. Remove foil and bake for another 20 minutes until casserole is bubbly and top is nicely browned.

Ingredients

1 pound chopped beef or pork

1 large onion, chopped

1/2 teaspoon fennel

Salt and pepper, to taste

1 loaf Italian bread, cut into 1/2-inch cubes

4 large zucchini, trimmed and sliced

1 cup shredded mozzarella

1/2 cup grated romano cheese

4 tablespoons butter

Submitted by:
Chris Fennimore, WQED Pittsburgh

From the Garden

America's
HOME COOKING
Tomatoes

Baked Green Tomatoes

DIRECTIONS

Preheat oven to 350 degrees. Cut tomatoes into slightly smaller than 1/2-inch slices and arrange half of them in a single layer in a greased baking dish. Scatter half of bread cubes on top, season with salt and pepper and dot with half of margarine; repeat, making a second layer. Sprinkle cheese on top. Bake uncovered for 45 to 50 minutes or until tender. Serves 6.

INGREDIENTS

8 medium green tomatoes

1 cup small bread cubes, toasted

1 1/2 teaspoons salt

1/8 teaspoon pepper

3 tablespoons margarine

1/3 cup grated parmesan cheese

SUBMITTED BY:
Lola Olinski, Maynard

Baked Whole Tomatoes

DIRECTIONS

Preheat oven to 375 degrees. Cut stem ends from tomatoes. Cut thin slices from top of each. Place tomatoes in a shallow pan; cut a cross about 1/2 inch deep in the top of each.

Sprinkle tomatoes with salt and pepper; spread with salad dressing and sprinkle with cheese. Bake for about 20 minutes, until tomato is thoroughly heated. Serves 6.

INGREDIENTS

6 medium tomatoes

1 teaspoon salt

1/8 teaspoon pepper

3/4 cup salad dressing

3 tablespoons grated sharp processed cheese

America's
HOME COOKING

SUBMITTED BY:
Lola Olinski, Maynard

Breaded Tomatoes with Cheese Sauce

DIRECTIONS

Preheat oven to 475 degrees. Peel and core tomatoes, leaving them whole. Dip each tomato in melted butter. In a small bowl, combine saltine crumbs and parmesan cheese. Roll tomatoes in crumb mixture, gently pressing crumbs onto tomato. Place tomatoes in a single layer in a greased, shallow baking dish. If any crumbs or butter are left, combine them and sprinkle over tomatoes. Bake for 15 minutes or until tomatoes begin to brown and are heated through. Watch closely as they burn easily.

To make cheese sauce, melt butter in saucepan. Stir in flour, salt and pepper. Add milk all at once. Cook and stir over medium heat until thickened and bubbly. Remove from heat and stir in parmesan cheese. Serve over tomatoes. Makes 8 to 10 servings.

INGREDIENTS

8 to 10 small to medium firm, fresh tomatoes

1/2 cup butter or margarine, melted

1 cup crushed saltines

1 tablespoon grated parmesan cheese

CHEESE SAUCE:

2 tablespoons butter or margarine

2 tablespoons all-purpose flour

1/4 teaspoon salt

Dash white pepper

1 1/2 cups milk

3 tablespoons grated parmesan cheese

SUBMITTED BY:
Julia Gyure, Daisytown

Bruchetti

DIRECTIONS

Toast Italian bread in toaster. Brush each slice of bread with olive oil, and then rub garlic clove over toast. Arrange tomato slices on toast and top with provolone cheese. Heat toast under broiler until cheese melts. Serves 4.

INGREDIENTS

4 slices Italian bread

Olive oil

1 clove garlic, sliced in half

2 plum tomatoes, sliced lengthwise

4 sliced provolone cheese

America's
HOME COOKING

SUBMITTED BY:
Diane Barnes, Fairmont

Carolyn's Country Garden Quiche

DIRECTIONS

Preheat oven to 450 degrees. Bake pie crust for 5 minutes. Line bottom with tomato slices. Fill in any empty spaces. Crumble feta cheese on top of tomatoes. Beat eggs in a bowl and mix in cream, hot pepper sauce and pepper. Pour mixture over feta and tomatoes. Bake for 15 minutes; reduce heat to 350 degrees. Continue baking for another 10 to 15 minutes or until a knife inserted 1 inch from the side comes out clean.

INGREDIENTS

1 (9-inch) pie crust

2 large tomatoes, cut into 1/4-inch-thick slices

1 (4-ounce) package basil and tomato feta cheese

2 eggs

1 cup heavy whipping cream

2 dashes hot pepper sauce

1/2 teaspoon black or white pepper

SUBMITTED BY:
Carolyn Fronapel

Crunchy Fried Tomatoes

DIRECTIONS

Wash tomatoes and cut into 3/4-inch slices. Dip slices into beaten egg and then into breadcrumbs. Melt margarine in a large skillet. Add tomato slices; cook, turning once, until golden brown. Season to taste.

INGREDIENTS

4 green medium tomatoes

1 egg, beaten

1 cup dry breadcrumbs

1/3 cup margarine

Salt and pepper, to taste

America's
HOME COOKING

SUBMITTED BY:
Lola Olinski, Maynard

Easy Pan Fried Tomatoes

DIRECTIONS

Wash tomatoes and cut into 3/4-inch slices. St r together flour, salt and pepper. Dip tomato slices into flour mixture, coating both sides. Melt margarine in large skillet. Add tomato slices and cook, turning once, until golden brown.

INGREDIENTS

4 green medium tomatoes

1/2 cup all-purpose flour

1 teaspoon salt

1/4 teaspoon pepper

1/3 cup margarine

SUBMITTED BY:
Lola Olinski, Maynard

Fire and Ice Tomatoes

DIRECTIONS

In a large bowl, combine tomatoes, onion, green pepper and cucumber. In a small saucepan, combine vinegar, water, sugar, celery salt, mustard seed, salt, cayenne pepper and black pepper. Bring to a boil over medium high heat; boil for 1 minute. Pour hot vinegar mixture over tomato mixture. Cover and refrigerate for 8 hours, or overnight, to let flavors blend. Serve with a slotted spoon.

INGREDIENTS

6 medium tomatoes, peeled and quartered

1 medium onion, sliced

1 medium green bell pepper, cut into strips

1 large cucumber, peeled and sliced

3/4 cup cider vinegar

1/4 cup water

1 tablespoon plus 2 teaspoons granulated sugar

1 1/2 teaspoons celery salt

1 1/2 teaspoons mustard seed

1/4 teaspoon salt

1/2 teaspoon cayenne pepper

1/8 teaspoon black pepper

America's
HOME COOKING

SUBMITTED BY:
Charlene Kula, Greensburg

Fried Green Tomatoes

DIRECTIONS

Wash tomatoes and pat dry. Slice into 1/2-inch slices. Combine flour, corn meal, salt, pepper and garlic powder. Place in a shallow bowl or plate. Heat oil or shortening in a frying pan. Coat each slice with flour mixture and shake off excess flour. Place into hot pan and brown on both sides. After tomatoes are brown, reduce heat and partially cover pan. Cook until tomatoes are tender.

To make a cream sauce, remove tomatoes from pan and add a little cream; heat until thickened. Serve sauce on side. Serves 6 to 8.

INGREDIENTS

6 to 8 large green tomatoes

1/2 cup flour

1/2 cup cornmeal

2 teaspoons salt

1 teaspoon black pepper

1/2 teaspoon garlic powder (optional)

1/2 cup cooking oil or shortening

Heavy cream (optional)

SUBMITTED BY:
Carolyn Moschak, Pittsburgh—Recipe from Oleta Steele, Grand Prairie

Jan's Good Tomato Recipe

DIRECTIONS

Line the bottom of a 9-inch pie or quiche pan with a single layer of croutons. Alternate tomato slices with mozzarella slices on top of croutons. Sprinkle with salad dressing and then basil.

Heat in a microwave oven for 5 to 8 minutes or until cheese has melted.

INGREDIENTS

1 (6-ounce) package garlic and cheese croutons

2 large tomatoes, sliced 1/4 inc thick

1/2 pound mozzarella cheese, sliced

4 tablespoons red wine vinegar salad dressing

1/2 teaspoon dried basil

America's
HOME COOKING

SUBMITTED BY:
Jan Herrle, Garfield

Mediterranean Tomato Salad

DIRECTIONS

Halve garlic and rub a large salad bowl with cut side; discard garlic. Combine tomatoes, olives and cheese in salad bowl. Add vinegar, oil, oregano and thyme; toss to mix well. Season salad with salt and pepper.

Cover and refrigerate at least 4 hours to allow flavors to blend. Let salad stand at room temperature for 1 or 2 hours before serving.

NOTE

If desired, drain some of the dressing before serving. Thoroughly drain leftovers before storing in refrigerator.

INGREDIENTS

1 clove garlic

3 large ripe tomatoes, cut into bite-size pieces

12 pitted black olives, halved

3/4 cup cubed feta cheese

3 tablespoons red wine vinegar

1/2 cup olive oil

1/2 teaspoon dried oregano

1/2 teaspoon dried thyme

Salt, to taste

Freshly ground black pepper, to taste

SUBMITTED BY:
Charlene Kula, Greensburg

Plum Tomato Tart

DIRECTIONS

Set oven rack on upper level; preheat to 400 degrees. Lightly coat a baking sheet with nonstick cooking spray or line with parchment paper. In a small bowl, whisk together egg white and olive oil. Lay a sheet of phyllo on prepared baking sheet and, with a pastry brush, lightly coat surface with egg-white mixture. Sprinkle with 1 teaspoon breadcrumbs. Repeat this step, layering 4 more sheets of phyllo on top. Lay the sixth sheet of phyllo on top and brush with egg-white mixture. To form an edge to the tart, carefully roll over the edges toward the center, using the blade of a knife to get started.

With a rubber spatula, spread mustard over the surface of the dough and sprinkle with cheese. The tart can be prepared ahead to this point. (Wrap and freeze for up to 2 months. Do not thaw before continuing.) Arrange tomato slices on top in 5 rows of 8 slices each. Bake for 15 to 20 minutes, or until pastry is golden brown. Let cook in the pan for 5 minutes. In a small bowl, combine basil, parsley and garlic. With fingers or a fork, dab some of the herb mixture onto each tomato slice. Slide tart onto a serving platter or, if you wish to serve bite-sized appetizers, slide it onto a cutting board and with a sharp knife or pizza cutter, cut the tart into squares between the tomato slices. Serve warm or at room temperature. Takes about 10 minutes to prepare. Makes 40 appetizers.

INGREDIENTS

1 large egg white

2 tablespoons olive oil

6 (14x8-inch) sheets phyllo dough

5 teaspoons fine dry breadcrumbs

1/3 cup Dijon mustard

1/4 cup freshly grated parmesan cheese

1 pound plum tomatoes (about 8), cored and sliced 1/4 inch thick

1 tablespoon fresh basil

2 tablespoons chopped fresh parsley

2 cloves garlic, finely chopped

America's HOME COOKING

SUBMITTED BY: Barbara Knezovich, McKeesport

Salsa

DIRECTIONS

Blanch and peel tomatoes. Remove seeds, if desired, and chop. Add remaining ingredients. Cook over medium heat until peppers, onions and celery are tender. Cool and serve with tortilla chips.

NOTE

Wear rubber gloves when handling jalapeños. Two peppers make a mild salsa; 8 a very hot salsa.

INGREDIENTS

6 medium tomatoes

1/2 stalk celery, finely chopped

1 medium onion, chopped

2 to 8 small fresh jalapeno peppers, chopped

1 tablespoon lime juice (optional)

1 teaspoon basil

1/2 teaspoon salt (optional)

SUBMITTED BY:
Mary Baden, Gibsonia

Scalloped Tomatoes

DIRECTIONS

Preheat oven to 350 degrees. Cook onion in butter until tender, but not brown; stir in crumbled bread. In a 1-quart casserole, layer half of tomatoes; sprinkle with salt, pepper and sugar, to taste. Cover tomatoes with half of bread mixture, repeat layers. Bake uncovered for 30 minutes. Serves 6.

INGREDIENTS

1 medium onion, chopped (about 1/2 cup)

1/4 cup butter

3 slices bread, coarsely crumbled (about 2 1/4 cups)

6 medium tomatoes, peeled and sliced

Salt, to taste

Pepper, to taste

Sugar, to taste

America's
HOME COOKING

SUBMITTED BY:
Reda Kirschman, Pittsburgh

Stewed Tomatoes

DIRECTIONS

Remove stem end from each tomato; peel and cut into small pieces. In medium saucepan, stir together all ingredients except bread cubes. Cover and heat to boiling; reduce heat and simmer 8 to 10 minutes. Stir in bread cubes and serve.

INGREDIENTS

3 large ripe tomatoes (about 1 1/2 pounds)

1/3 cup finely chopped onion

2 tablespoons chopped green pepper

1 tablespoon sugar

1/2 teaspoon salt

1/8 teaspoon pepper

1 cup soft bread cubes

SUBMITTED BY:
Lola Olinski, Maynard

35

Tomato and Cheese Strata

DIRECTIONS

Heat olive oil and sauté onion, garlic and green pepper for 5 minutes. Add tomatoes, tomato paste, spices (except dry mustard) and chilies to mixture. Simmer for 10 minutes. In a buttered 9x13-inch pan, layer half of the bread, tomato sauce and cheese, and then finish with remaining bread and cheese. Mix eggs with milk and dry mustard and pour over casserole. Cover and refrigerate overnight. Bake at 350 degrees for 50 minutes. Serves 8.

INGREDIENTS

2 teaspoons olive oil

2 onions, minced

2 cloves garlic, minced

2 green peppers, minced

12 medium tomatoes, peeled and sliced

1 (6-ounce) can tomato paste

Cayenne, salt, pepper, parsley and oregano, to taste

3 (4-ounce) cans peeled and diced green chilies

16 slices French bread, buttered and cubed

1/2 pound cheddar cheese, grated

6 eggs

4 cups milk

2 teaspoons dry mustard

America's
HOME COOKING

SUBMITTED BY:
Susan Mihalo VanRiper, Allison Park

Tomato Fans

Directions

Combine cottage cheese, provolone and parmesan cheese, oil, garlic, salt and pepper in a bowl, mix thoroughly. Cut each tomato vertically into 6 slices without cutting through bottom. Spoon 1 heaping teaspoon of cheese mixture between each slice. Cover and chill for 1 hour. Cut spinach into thin strips. Serve tomatoes on spinach.

Ingredients

1/4 cup cottage cheese

1/3 cup shredded provolone cheese

2 tablespoons grated parmesan cheese

2 tablespoons olive oil

1 small clove garlic, minced

1/4 teaspoon salt

1/8 teaspoon pepper

6 small ripe tomatoes

6 spinach leaves, for serving

SUBMITTED BY:
Charlene Kula, Greensburg

Tomato Pie

DIRECTIONS

Preheat oven to 350 degrees. Bake crust for about 10 minutes or until brown. Layer tomatoes in crust and then sprinkle with onions, basil, salt and pepper. Repeat layers until crust is full. Mix mayonnaise and cheese and spread over top. Bake for 30 minutes or until brown and bubbly. Makes 5 to 6 servings.

INGREDIENTS

1 (9-inch) deep dish pie crust

3 to 4 large ripe tomatoes, thickly sliced

1/2 cup finely chopped onions

Basil, salt and pepper, to taste

1 cup mayonnaise

1 cup grated sharp cheddar cheese

America's
HOME COOKING

SUBMITTED BY:
Paula Sullivan, Pittsburgh

Tomatoes Oregonata

DIRECTIONS

Cut tomatoes into approximately 1-inch cubes. Crush garlic with the back of a knife and add to tomatoes along with other ingredients. Stir with a wooden spoon and refrigerate for at least 4 hours. Serve with some nice crusty French or Italian bread to soak up the juice that forms.

INGREDIENTS

6 medium tomatoes or
12 plum tomatoes

1 clove garlic

1/4 cup olive oil

1 1/2 teaspoons salt

1/2 teaspoon fresh black pepper

1 1/2 tablespoons oregano

1 tablespoon fresh basil,
if available

French or Italian bread,
for serving

SUBMITTED BY:
Chris Fennimore, WQED Pittsburgh

Yellow Tomato Coulis

DIRECTIONS

Sauté garlic and shallots until tender. Add tomatoes and white wine. Simmer until softened and saucy. Transfer to a blender or food processor, add a little olive oil and blend until smooth. Strain through a sieve, pressing on solids. (You can also serve it rustic style, just do not sieve.) Garnish dish with halved yellow tomatoes and basil leaves.

INGREDIENTS

1 to 2 cloves garlic, finely chopped

1 to 2 shallots, finely chopped

1 pound yellow pear or cherry tomatoes (about 2 2/3 cups), reserve some for garnishing

1/4 cup white wine

1/4 teaspoon each salt and pepper

Olive oil

Basil leaves, for garnishing

America's
HOME COOKING

SUBMITTED BY:
Carrleen Kemble, Pittsburgh

FROM THE GARDEN

America's
HOME COOKING
ZUCCHINI

Grilled Zucchini with Feta

DIRECTIONS

Wash zucchini and slice lengthwise into 1/2-inch slices. Brush with salad dressing and grill at medium until just softened, about 5 minutes per side. Remove to a platter and sprinkle with feta. Serve with any grilled meat.

NOTE

This recipe is a great way to use those baseball bat-sized zucchinis.

INGREDIENTS

2 large zucchini

1/2 cup Italian salad dressing

1/2 cup crumbled feta cheese

SUBMITTED BY:
K mberlee Love, Sewickley

Mock Crab Cakes

Directions

Mix all ingredients well. Press into cakes and brown in margarine or butter.

Note

This really does taste like crab cakes!

Ingredients

2 cups grated zucchini

2 tablespoons grated onions

2 tablespoons grated celery

1 tablespoon salad dressing

1 tablespoon Old Bay seasonin

2 eggs

2 cups very fine and very dry breadcrumbs

Margarine or butter

America's
HOME COOKING

SUBMITTED BY:
Jean Bolyard, Westover

Stuffed Zucchini Boats

DIRECTIONS

Preheat oven to 350 degrees. Cook rice in water until done; set aside. Wash zucchini thoroughly, trim ends and slice in half length-wise. Scoop out pulp, leaving a 1/4-inch shell. Chop zucchini pulp and reserve for later use. Sauté onion and garlic in oil until softened. Add chopped zucchini, red or green pepper, mushrooms, herbs, spices and salt, and cook until zucchini is softened. Remove from heat, add tomatoes and rice and mix well.

Spoon rice-vegetable mixture into zucchini shells. Place zucchini in a baking dish that has 1/4 inch of water in bottom. Cover and bake for 20 minutes. Uncover and bake an additional 10 minutes or until zucchini is tender.

INGREDIENTS

1/2 cup brown rice, uncooked

1 1/2 cups water

2 medium zucchini

1 tablespoon oil

1 small onion, chopped

2 cloves garlic, minced

1 red or green pepper, diced

1/2 cup mushrooms, chopped

1 teaspoon Italian seasoning

Dash cayenne pepper

1/4 teaspoon black pepper

1/4 cup fresh chopped parsley

1/4 teaspoon salt

2 tomatoes, chopped

10 pimento/stuffed green olives, sliced

SUBMITTED BY:
Vi Scaringi, Verona

Zucchini Cheesecake

DIRECTIONS

Preheat oven to 350 degrees. Mix all ingredients together except squash. Squeeze out excess moisture from squash and fold in with other ingredients. Bake in a greased 8x8-inch casserole dish for about 30 minutes.

INGREDIENTS

1 cup baking mix

1/4 cup finely chopped onion

1 clove garlic, crushed

1/2 cup grated romano cheese

1 tablespoon chopped parsley

1/2 teaspoon oregano

1/2 teaspoon salt and pepper

1/2 cup olive oil

4 eggs

2 medium squash, shredded and drained

America's
HOME COOKING

SUBMITTED BY:
Mary Ann Fennimore Sr., Coral Springs

Zucchini Flowers with Goat Cheese and Mint

DIRECTIONS

Preheat oven to 350 degrees. Lightly beat egg, crumble in goat cheese and mash together with a fork. Add salt, pepper and mint. Stuff each of zucchini flowers with a small amount of cheese mixture and twist to close. Cover a baking sheet with aluminum foil. Pour a small amount of olive oil on the sheet and spread it around. Roll stuffed flowers through oil until lightly coated. Bake for 12 to 15 minutes, until lightly browned and fragrant.

NOTE

These delicate, bright flowers have a surprisingly concentrated zucchini flavor. In Italy, they are often stuffed with ricotta and fried.

INGREDIENTS

1 egg

3 ounces fresh goat cheese

Salt and pepper, to taste

2 teaspoons packed, chopped fresh mint

12 zucchini flowers

Olive oil

SUBMITTED BY:
Friend of WQED Pittsburgh

Zucchini Fritters

DIRECTIONS

Mix all ingredients except flour and oil. Add flour and oil. Drop by teaspoonful into preheated pan with vegetable or olive oil. Lightly fry on both sides until golden brown.

INGREDIENTS

2 cups grated zucchini

1/2 cup grated romano cheese

1/2 cup freshly chopped parsley

2 eggs beaten

1 teaspoon salt

Dash pepper

3/4 to 1 cup flour

1 teaspoon oil

America's
HOME COOKING

SUBMITTED BY:
Joseph S. Certo, Forest Hills

Zucchini Pancakes

DIRECTIONS

Using the large holes on a box grater, grate zucchini; place in a medium bowl. Add salt, pepper, eggs, parmesan, onion and garlic; mix well. Slowly add flour, stirring to insure no lumps form. Heat 2 tablespoons of oil in a large skillet over medium-high heat. Drop about 3 tablespoons of zucchini mixture into pan for each pancake. Cook 2 to 3 minutes. Lower heat to medium and turn pancakes over. Garnish with fresh parsley and serve with sour cream.

INGREDIENTS

2 medium zucchini
(about 1 pound)

1/2 teaspoon salt

1/4 teaspoon ground pepper

2 eggs, lightly beaten

1/2 cup grated parmesan cheese

1/4 cup grated onion

1 medium clove garlic, peeled and finely minced

3/4 cup flour

2 to 4 tablespoons corn or canola oil

Fresh parsley, for garnishing

Sour cream, for serving

SUBMITTED BY:
Helen Skalski

Zucchini Parmesan

DIRECTIONS

Set out a 2-quart casserole and a 3-quart sauce pan with a tight-fitting cover.

Wash, trim off ends and cut zucchini crosswise into 1/8-inch slices. In sauce pan, heat olive oil, and add zucchini, onions and mushrooms. Cover saucepan and cook zucchini mixture over low heat for 10 to 15 minutes or until tender, occasionally turning and moving mixture with a spoon. Remove zucchini mixture from heat; mix in about 1/2 of grated cheese with fork.

Preheat oven to 350 degrees. Mix together tomato paste, salt, garlic salt/garlic clove and pepper, and pour into saucepan. Blend lightly and thoroughly, pour into casserole and sprinkle with remaining cheese. Bake for 20 to 30 minutes.

INGREDIENTS

8 to 10 small zucchini squash (about 2 1/2 pounds)

3 tablespoons olive oil

2/3 cup coarsely chopped onions

1/4 pound sliced mushrooms

2/3 cup grated parmesan cheese (about 3 ounces)

2 (6-ounce) cans tomato paste (about 1 1/2 cups)

1 teaspoon salt

1/2 teaspoon garlic salt or 1 clove garlic, minced

1/8 teaspoon pepper

America's
HOME COOKING

SUBMITTED BY:
Vi Scaringi, Verona

Zucchini Quiche

DIRECTIONS

In a large skillet, sauté zucchini and onion in butter until tender; drain. Preheat oven to 400 degrees. In a large bowl, whisk eggs, parsley, salt, pepper and spices together. Stir in cheese and zucchini mixture and blend. Spread mustard with a pastry brush over bottom of pie shell, and add zucchini mixture. Bake uncovered for 35 to 40 minutes or until knife inserted near the center comes out clean and crust is golden (cover loosely with foil after 25 minutes, if needed, to prevent over browning.) Let stand for 10 minutes before cutting.

NOTE

Cover and freeze before baking. Quiche can be frozen for up to two months. To bake, thaw in refrigerator and bake, uncovered, at 400 degrees for 50 to 55 minutes. Cover with foil after 35 minutes.

INGREDIENTS

4 heaping cups sliced zucchini

1 large onion, thinly sliced

3 tablespoons butter

2 eggs

2 teaspoons dry parsley flakes

1/2 teaspoon salt

1/4 teaspoon pepper

1/2 teaspoon garlic powder

1/2 teaspoon dried basil

1/2 teaspoon oregano

2 cups shredded mozzarella

2 teaspoons Dijon mustard

1 (9-inch) pastry shell

SUBMITTED BY:
Dorothy Rozzolla, Indiana

Zucchini Stuffing Casserole

DIRECTIONS

Preheat oven to 350 degrees.

Cook zucchini in a little salted, boiling water until tender; drain. In a saucepan, cook carrots and onion in 4 teaspoons of butter or margarine until tender. Remove from heat; stir in 1 1/2 cups of stuffing cubes, soup and sour cream. Stir in zucchini gently. Turn into 1 1/2-quart casserole.

Melt remaining butter or margarine; add remaining stuffing cubes. Toss gently until coated and add to top of casserole.

Bake for 30 to 40 minutes. Serves 6 to 8.

INGREDIENTS

4 medium zucchini, cubed

3/4 cup shredded carrots

1/2 cup chopped onion

6 tablespoons margarine or butter

2 1/4 cups herbed stuffing cubes

1 (10 3/4-ounce) can cream of chicken soup

1/2 cup sour cream

America's
HOME COOKING

SUBMITTED BY:
Mary Sullivan, Beaver

FROM THE GARDEN

America's
HOME COOKING
MIXED VEGETABLES

Asparagus and Red Pepper Sauté

DIRECTIONS

Warm olive oil in skillet. Add asparagus, red pepper, salt and pepper. Sauté until tender, but crisp. Add vinegar and mix. Remove from heat. Transfer to a serving dish. Cool slightly and sprinkle with parmesan.

INGREDIENTS

2 tablespoons olive oil

1 pound asparagus, cut in 1-inch pieces

1 large red pepper, cut in 1-inch pieces

1/2 teaspoon salt

1/4 teaspoon black pepper

1 tablespoon red wine vinegar

1/4 teaspoon parmesan

SUBMITTED BY:
Ruth E. Platek, Robinson Township

Broccoli Stir Fry

DIRECTIONS

In a skillet over medium-high heat, stir fry broccoli in butter and lemon-pepper until crisp tender, about 2 to 3 minutes.

INGREDIENTS

3 cups fresh broccoli florets

1/4 cup butter

1 1/2 teaspoons lemon pepper seasoning

SUBMITTED BY:
Karen Coursin, Waynesburg

56

Corn and Basil Egg Roulade

Directions

Preheat oven to 325 degrees. Butter a
15 1/2x11-inch jelly roll pan and line bottom and
sides with parchment paper. Chop scallions and
basil, keep separated. In a large bowl, whisk
together eggs, heavy cream and salt until well
combined. Whisk in parmesan reggiano cheese.
Pour custard into jelly roll pan and bake in the
middle of oven for 8 to 10 minutes. Rotate pan and
continue to bake for an additional 8 to 10 minutes.
Chill in refrigerator.

While custard is baking, in a heavy skillet, heat
butter over moderately low heat and cook scallions,
stirring until softened, about 2 to 3 minutes.
Cut cream cheese into small pieces and add to
scallions. Spoon in mascarpone. Add corn and salt
and pepper to taste. Cook mixture, stirring until corn
is heated through and cream cheese is melted,
about 2 to 3 minutes. Turn off heat and add basil.
Cool mixture and egg sheet a little in a freezer
or refrigerator. With long side facing you, spread
corn mixture evenly on top of egg sheet, leaving a
1-inch border on all sides. Using parchment paper
as a rolling aid, roll up egg sheet jelly-roll style and
carefully transfer to a platter. Dish can be reheated
on a parchment-lined baking sheet either whole or
cut in slices, or it can be served at room temperature
with yellow tomato coulis and black forest ham
slices.

Submitted by:
Carrleen Kemble, Pittsburgh

Ingredients

1 bunch scallions

1 cup packed fresh basil leaves

6 large eggs

2 cups heavy cream

1/2 teaspoon salt

1/2 cup parmesan reggiano
cheese

2 tablespoons unsalted butter

1/4 cup cream cheese (about 2
ounces)

1/4 cup mascarpone cheese

1/4 teaspoon pepper

2 cups fresh (or thawed, frozen)
corn kernels

Corn and Rock Shrimp Pot Pie

DIRECTIONS

Preheat oven to 450 degrees. Heat butter in a large sauce pan over medium heat. When melted, add leeks and garlic. Cook, stirring, about 4 minutes. Add bay leaves, nutmeg, cayenne and flour. Cook for 1 minute. Add corn and thyme, and cook for 1 minute more. Stir in stock and cream. Cook until liquid is thickened and reduced by 2/3, about 7 to 8 minutes. Add shrimp. Cook until pink, about 2 minutes. Remove from heat, and discard bay leaves. Season with salt and pepper. (1/4 cup dry sherry wine can be added as well.) Place in ramekins or baking dish. Using fingers, place small blobs of biscuit dough on top. Bake until crust is golden brown and cooked through, about 12 minutes.

NOTE

This recipe is for individual servings made in heat-proof bowls or ramekins. 1 (8-inch) square baking dish also can be used.

INGREDIENTS

3 tablespoons unsalted butter

3 leeks, white part only, cleaned and chopped

1 to 2 cloves garlic, minced

2 bay leaves

1/4 teaspoon nutmeg

1/4 teaspoon cayenne pepper

1 tablespoon all-purpose flour

6 ears corn (about 6 cups)

1 teaspoon thyme leaves

1 1/4 cups homemade or low-sodium canned chicken stock

1 cup heavy cream

1 pound rock shrimp, peeled and deveined

Salt, to taste

Cornmeal biscuit dough (See page 59 for recipe)

America's
HOME COOKING

SUBMITTED BY:
Carrleen Kemble, Pittsburgh

Cornmeal Biscuit Dough

DIRECTIONS

In a bowl, whisk flour, cornmeal, baking powder, baking soda, salt and sugar. Using fingers or a pastry cutter, cut butter into flour mixture. Using a wooden spoon, stir in buttermilk until dough holds together. Use immediately.

INGREDIENTS

1 1/2 cups all-purpose flour

1/4 cup plus 2 tablespoons yellow cornmeal

2 teaspoons baking powder

3/4 teaspoon baking soda

1/4 teaspoon salt

1 1/2 tablespoons sugar

6 tablespoons chilled butter, cut into 1/2-inch pieces

1/4 cup nonfat buttermilk

SUBMITTED BY:
Carrleen Kemble, Pittsburgh

Gazpacho I

Combine ingredients and refrigerate. Serves 6 to 8.

INGREDIENTS

1/2 cup diced celery

1/2 cup diced green pepper

1/2 cup diced onion

1/2 cup diced cucumber

1/2 cup diced tomatoes

1 (10 3/4-ounce) can tomato soup

1 (10 3/4-ounce) can water

1 tablespoon Italian dressing

1/2 teaspoon black pepper

1 dash Worchestershire sauce

1 1/2 cups wine vinegar

1 tablespoon garlic powder

4 dashes hot sauce

America's
HOME COOKING

SUBMITTED BY:
Nancy Polinsky, WQED Pittsburgh

Glazed Carrots

DIRECTIONS

In a saucepan, cook carrots in a small amount of water until crisp tender. Drain carrots and keep warm. In the same pan, heat brown sugar and butter until bubbly. Stir in lemon peel. Return carrots to the pan; cook and stir over low heat for 10 to 15 minutes or until glazed. Remove from heat. Stir in vanilla and serve.

INGREDIENTS

12 medium carrots, cut in 1-inch pieces

1/2 cup packed brown sugar

3 tablespoons butter

1 tablespoon grated lemon peel

1/4 teaspoon vanilla extract

SUBMITTED BY:
Karen Coursin, Waynesburg

Haricots Verts in Walnut Oil

DIRECTIONS

Heat oils in a large skillet. Add green beans and stir to coat. Cook at a low sizzle for 3 minutes, stirring constantly. Season with salt. Cover with lid slightly ajar and cook for 6 minutes more, stirring every 2 minutes or so. Add more salt and pepper, to taste. Serve warm or at room temperature.

NOTE

Ordinary green beans can be used in place of haricots verts. If you have any leftovers, eat them topped with big chunks of tuna or a poached egg.

INGREDIENTS

1 tablespoon olive oil

2 tablespoons walnut oil

1 1/2 pounds haricots verts (extra-slim French green beans with tops trimmed

Salt and pepper

America's
HOME COOKING

SUBMITTED BY:
A Friend of WQED Pittsburgh

Mediterranean Fish with Fennel and Kalamata Olives

DIRECTIONS

To make kalamata cream, sauté shallot in olive oil. Add white wine, olives, olive juice and sugar; reduce to au sec (almost dry). Add heavy cream and reduce to slightly thickened consistency (should coat the back of a spoon. Hold sauce for service.

To cook fish, preheat oven to 350 degrees. Sauté fillets in a nonstick, oven-ready pan with olive oil. Turn and add white wine, fumet and lemon; place in oven to finish cooking, about 7 to 10 minutes.

Sauté fennel in olive oil over medium-high heat. Add garlic and sauté—when fennel begins to caramelize, add some white wine to steam. Add spinach and campanelli tomatoes, toss just to warm through, lightly season with salt and pepper.

Serve fish over fennel mixture, drizzled with kalamata cream and garnish with fennel leaves.

INGREDIENTS

1 shallot, chopped

Olive oil

White wine

1/3 cup kalamata olives, halved

3 tablespoons olive juice

1 to 2 tablespoons white or brown sugar

1 cup heavy cream

4 white fish fillets, such as striped bass, halibut or orange roughy

Fish fumet

1 lemon

2 fennel bulbs, thinly sliced

2 cloves garlic, chopped

9 ounces fresh spinach

1 (5-ounce) package campanelli tomatoes

Salt and pepper, to taste

SUBMITTED BY:
Chef Steven Hughes

Mixed Vegetables

DIRECTIONS

In a skillet, sauté celery, onion and garlic in butter until tender. Add broth, potatoes, carrots and pepper. Bring to a boil, reduce heat, cover and simmer for 15 to 20 minutes or until broth has thickened slightly, stirring occasionally. Sprinkle with parsley.

INGREDIENTS

1 cup sliced celery

1/2 cup chopped onion

2 garlic cloves, minced

3 tablespoons butter

1 1/2 cups chicken broth

4 cups cubed potatoes

1 cup julienne carrots

1/4 teaspoon pepper

1 tablespoon chopped fresh parsley

America's
HOME COOKING

SUBMITTED BY:
Karen Coursin, Waynesburg

Old Stone Inn Corn Fritters

DIRECTIONS

Cut corn from cob, making 1 1/2 to 2 cups kernels. Scrape cobs to extract milk. Mash 1/3 cup of corn pulp with a potato masher or blender. Return it to rest of corn. Mix egg yolks with corn. Sift together flour, cayenne pepper, sugar, salt and baking powder. Add to corn and mix well. Beat egg whites until stiff (not dry and grainy). Fold into corn. Heat fresh oil in a deep fryer at 375 degrees. Drop batter by tablespoonfuls into oil. Cook until browned, about 2 minutes. Turn if needed. Remove, drain and serve.

INGREDIENTS

6 fresh ears corn

3 eggs, separated

3/4 cup sifted all-purpose flour

Cayenne pepper, to taste

1 teaspoon sugar

1 teaspoon salt

2 teaspoons baking powder

Vegetable oil, for frying

SUBMITTED BY:
Kathy Geiger, Pittsburgh

Pesto Chicken

DIRECTIONS

Butterfly cut each chicken breast to create a very thin fillet. Pound each lightly with a mallet or the side of a large knife. Spread each fillet with 1 tablespoon pesto and roll up, tucking in sides as it is rolled. Close edge with toothpicks or tie each bundle with kitchen twine. Heat olive oil in a 10-inch fry pan and brown chicken breasts quickly on all sides. Remove chicken from pan and add butter and flour to form a roux. Stir it over medium-high heat, scraping any bits and pieces of chicken from bottom of the pan. Add wine and lemon juice and stir until mixture comes to a boil. Return chicken to pan, add salt and pepper, cover and let simmer for about 30 minutes. Serve with rice, buttered noodles or orzo (rice-shaped pasta).

NOTE

You can also slice these and serve at room temperature for a buffet.

INGREDIENTS

6 boneless chicken breasts

6 tablespoons pesto

2 tablespoons olive oil

1 tablespoon unsalted butter, softened

1 tablespoon flour

1 cup dry white wine

Juice of 1 lemon

Salt and pepper, to taste

America's
HOME COOKING

SUBMITTED BY:
Chris Fennimore, WQED Pittsburgh

Roasted Ratatouille

DIRECTIONS

Preheat oven to 350 degrees. Put 2 heads of garlic into a foil wrap after removing their bottoms, drizzle olive oil over garlic and wrap; bake for 1 hour.

Slice and cut vegetables into large, but bite-size pieces and place on a cookie sheet. Drizzle generously with olive oil, sprinkle with sea salt and fresh cracked black pepper, cover with a foil tent and roast in oven for about 1 hour.

Boil water for pasta of your choosing.

Remove garlic from oven and let cool. Put tomato paste into a sauce pan. Squeeze roasted garlic paste into tomato paste and stir with a wire whisk. Add about 2 cups of pasta water to tomato-garlic sauce and whisk; set aside.

Prepare pasta and place in a bowl and toss with 1/8 cup tomato sauce and olive oil.

Remove roasted vegetables from oven and place nto pasta, cover with garlic tomato sauce. Garnish with fresh basil. Toss and serve. Bon appetite!

NOTE

Eggplant, peppers and zucchini flavors blend well for this dish and make a taste all their own when roasted together.

INGREDIENTS

Select various fresh eggplants; zucchini; onions; green, red and yellow peppers; tomatoes; and garlic

Olive oil

Sea salt and fresh cracked black pepper, to taste

Pasta, for serving

1 to 2 (6-ounce) cans tomato paste

Fresh basil, for garnishing

SUBMITTED BY:
Renee A. Reiland, paralegal, Edgar Snyder & Associates

Skillet Vegetables

DIRECTIONS

In a skillet, combine oil and salad dressing mix. Add carrots and cook over medium heat for 4 to 5 minutes or until crisp tender. Add squash and zucchini and cook for another 4 to 5 minutes or until all vegetables are tender.

INGREDIENTS

1 tablespoon cooking oil

1 (1-ounce) envelope buttermilk ranch salad dressing mix

2 medium carrots, thinly sliced

2 medium yellow squash, sliced

2 medium zucchini, sliced

America's
HOME COOKING

SUBMITTED BY:
Karen Coursin, Waynesburg

Stuffed Fried Cubanella Sweet Peppers

DIRECTIONS

Cut tops off peppers and clean out seeds. Mix all ingredients except eggs and olive oil in a large bowl. Beat eggs with olive oil in a small bowl. Pour egg and oil mixture over dry ingredients and stir. Stuff mixture into peppers. Fry peppers slowly in additional olive oil over low heat turning frequently to brown all sides.

INGREDIENTS

12 to 18 cubanella peppers

2 cups seasoned breadcrumbs

1/2 cup chopped black olives

1/2 cup chopped green stuffed olives

2 to 3 plum tomatoes, seeded and chopped

1 cup asiago cheese

1/2 cup grated romano cheese

2 eggs

1/4 cup olive oil plus additional oil for frying

SUBMITTED BY:
Joseph S. Certo, Forest Hills

Succotash

DIRECTIONS

In a large skillet, cook bacon until crisp. Remove bacon to paper towels. Drain fat from pan, reserving 1 tablespoon of drippings. Add corn, beans, green pepper and onion to drippings. Simmer for 10 to 15 minutes or until vegetables are almost tender. Add water if necessary. Stir in tomatoes and bacon. Cook just until tomatoes are heated.

INGREDIENTS

1/4 pound sliced bacon, diced

2 cups fresh corn

1/2 pound lima beans

1 medium green pepper, chopped

1 medium onion, chopped

2 medium tomatoes, cut in wedges

America's
HOME COOKING

SUBMITTED BY:
Karen Coursin, Waynesburg

Swiss Chard, Beans and Tomatoes

DIRECTIONS

Thoroughly wash Swiss chard. Remove stems and tear remaining leaves into bite-sized pieces. Steam chard and onions in a large pot or wok with only the water remaining on leaves after washing. When chard has collapsed, add tomatoes, olive oil, vinegar, garlic and shallots. Continue to steam for 5 to 8 minutes. Add beans with their liquid and season to taste.

Serve with bread and thin slices of pecorino romano cheese. Serves 6.

INGREDIENTS

5 large bunches Swiss chard

2 medium onions, chopped

6 tomatoes, peeled, seeded and chopped

1/4 cup olive oil

1/4 cup balsamic vinegar

2 cloves garlic, crushed

2 large shallots, chopped fine

1 (16-ounce) can cannellini beans

Salt and pepper, to taste

Pecorino romano cheese, sliced thinly for serving

SUBMITTED BY:
Susan Mihalo VanRiper, Allison Park

From the Garden

America's
Home Cooking
Eggplant

Crepes

DIRECTIONS

Put all ingredients in a blender and process at a medium speed until smooth. Heat a nonstick 10-inch crepe pan or frying pan and coat it with nonstick cooking spray. It is important to heat pan until it is hot, but spray does not burn. Add about 1/3 cup batter starting at one end of the pan and tipping pan quickly to coat entire surface. The edges will start to dry out and batter will get less shiny as it cooks quickly. Turn crepe by lifting edge with a spatula and flipping it over with your fingers. Heat second side for about 30 seconds and place on a plate. Continue process of spraying pan, adding batter and quickly tipping it to coat evenly, cooking on both sides until all the batter is used. Crepes can be stored in the refrigerator covered with plastic wrap for a few days.

INGREDIENTS

3 eggs

1/2 cup milk

1/2 cup water

1 cup flour

3 tablespoons sugar

SUBMITTED BY:
Nancy Weinstein

Eggplant Pizza

DIRECTIONS

Preheat oven to 450 degrees. Fry diced eggplant in olive oil until soft cooked and slightly brown. Drain oil well and brush entire pizza crust with oil. Toss tomatoes, garlic, eggplant, onion, basil, salt, pepper and oregano well and spread evenly over crust. Top with cheese and place in oven for about 10 minutes or until cheese melts and is bubbly and crust is light brown on the bottom.

INGREDIENTS

1 medium eggplant, peeled and cut into large dice

1/2 cup olive oil

1 pizza crust, homemade or store-bought

3 medium fresh tomatoes, diced

1 clove garlic, crushed well

1 green onion, finely chopped

Fresh basil (about 10 to 15 leaves), rolled and sliced in shreds

Salt, pepper or red pepper flakes, to taste

1/2 teaspoon oregano

1 cup or more grated romano or parmesan mixed with mozzarella or any soft melting Italian cheese

America's
HOME COOKING

SUBMITTED BY:
Nina Mule' Lyons, North Hills

Eggplant Pudding

DIRECTIONS

Preheat oven to 350 degrees. Cook eggplant in boiling water to cover until tender, about 15 minutes. Drain thoroughly. Stir in remaining ingredients and pour into a well greased 1-quart casserole. Bake for about 1 hour until firm and well browned. Serves 5.

INGREDIENTS

1 medium eggplant, peeled and diced

2 well-beaten eggs

1 teaspoon salt

1 cup milk

3 tablespoons melted butter

2 cups soft breadcrumbs

SUBMITTED BY:
Christine Crighton, Crighton Farm

Fesenjan-e Bademjan

DIRECTIONS

Peel eggplants and remove stems. Salt and let sit for at least 20 minutes; rinse and squeeze out water. Slice into 1-inch rounds. Heat 4 tablespoons oil in deep skillet over medium heat. Add eggplant and sauté on all sides, about 15 minutes, until golden brown. Remove from skillet and drain; set aside. Add remaining oil to skillet and reheat over medium heat. Add onion and sauté until golden brown; add garlic to pan for last few minutes of cooking. Add cumin, cardamom, salt, pepper, turmeric, crushed red pepper, parsley, cilantro (or basil or oregano) and mint; Sauté for 5 minutes. Remove from heat and set aside. Grind walnuts until very fine (must be very fine in order to thicken sauce). Combine walnuts with pomegranate juice and honey, as needed, and stir until smooth.

Pour sauce into skillet. Return eggplants and seasoning to skillet, reduce heat to low, cover and simmer mixture for 30 minutes or until eggplants are tender, stirring occasionally with a wooden spoon. If sauce is too sour, add more honey or brown sugar to taste. Spoon onto serving dish or plates, and garnish with herb leaves and pomegranate seeds, and a dollop of yogurt. Serve with couscous or rice, warm flat bread and a fresh green salad.

NOTE

Fesenjan, the pomegranate and walnut sauce that gives this dish its tart taste, is usually prepared with chicken, but when I first enjoyed it in Isfehan, eggplant was the key ingredient. Some recipes combine chicken and eggplant.

INGREDIENTS

2 large eggplants

6 tablespoons olive oil

1 medium onion, peeled and sliced

2 cloves garlic, peeled and chopped

2 teaspoons ground cumin

1/4 teaspoon ground cardamom

2 teaspoons salt

1 teaspoon freshly ground pepper

1/2 teaspoon ground turmeric

1 teaspoon crushed red pepper

1 cup chopped fresh parsley

2 cups chopped fresh cilantro, lemon basil or oregano

1/2 cups chopped fresh mint

2 cups walnuts (about 1/2 pound)

3 cups pomegranate juice

1 tablespoon honey

Basmati rice, for serving

Yoghurt, for garnishing

America's
HOME COOKING

SUBMITTED BY:
Florence Wyand, Allegheny West

Ratatouille

DIRECTIONS

Preheat oven to 325 degrees. Heat oil in a large skillet. Crush or mince garlic, slice onions and add them both to oil. Sauté until onion is transparent. While onion is cooking, slice squash into rounds, cut peppers into strips and peel and cube eggplant. Dredge vegetable pieces lightly in flour. Put onion and garlic into a Dutch oven or large casserole. Add more oil to skillet if necessary and brown vegetables at medium-high heat. Add vegetables to onions. Cover and bake for approximately 1 hour. Finally, blanch and peel tomatoes and slice into mixture. Bake, uncovered, for another 30 minutes. Season with salt and pepper, and add capers during last 15 minutes of cooking. Serve this dish hot or cold with plenty of French bread.

INGREDIENTS

1/3 cup olive oil
2 cloves garlic
1 large onion
2 well-scrubbed zucchini
2 green peppers
1 small eggplant
3 tablespoons flour
5 ripe tomatoes
Salt and pepper, to taste
1 tablespoon capers
French bread, for serving

SUBMITTED BY:
Chris Fennimore, WQED Pittsburgh

Ratatouille Crepes

DIRECTIONS

In a large heavy pot, heat oil and add onion and pepper. Sauté until vegetables are soft, but not browned. Add garlic and continue cooking for about 1 minute—do not let garlic brown. Add zucchini and eggplant and stir until vegetables are well mixed. Add parsley and basil, mixing well. Add tomatoes, including liquid. Add a few grindings of pepper and salt, if desired. Stir all ingredients together and bring to a boil. Cover pot and lower flame to simmer for about 30 minutes until all vegetables are cooked down, but still firm and flavors are well blended. Every 7 to 8 minutes, remove liquid that accumulates in the pot with a bulb baster and put it in a small sauce pot. Remove vegetables from heat. Meanwhile, boil liquid in a small sauce pot briskly until it reduces to about 2 or 3 tablespoons of glaze. Pour it over the vegetables before serving.

NOTE

Ratatouille can be served warm or cold as a side dish or a main dish rolled in crepes. Serve with a salad made with Boston or butter crunch lettuce and a Dijon vinaigrette dressing.

INGREDIENTS

1/4 cup olive oil

1 1/2 cups sliced onion

1 large green pepper, seeded and sliced

1 teaspoon minced garlic

1 large or 2 small zucchini, sliced into 1/4-inch rounds

1 large eggplant, peeled and cut into 1-inch chunks

1/4 cup finely chopped parsley

1 tablespoon finely chopped fresh basil

1 pound tomatoes, diced, or 1 (14 1/2-ounce) can diced tomatoes, undrained

Fresh ground pepper and salt, to taste (optional)

Crepes (see page 75 for recipe) for serving (optional)

America's
HOME COOKING

SUBMITTED BY:
Nancy Weinstein

Summer Ratatouille

Directions

Heat oil over medium heat in a very large frying pan; add onions. Sauté, stirring occasionally, until onions are wilted and just beginning to color, about 25 minutes. (Don't rush this part as onions need to caramelize and sweeten.) Add eggplant. Stir to coat and sauté for 10 minutes. Add peppers. (The heat may be lowered at this point.) Sauté for 10 minutes. (The peppers will release some juice, which will start the sauce.) Add zucchini and sauté for 10 minutes. Add tomatoes and fresh thyme. Heat until tomatoes release some juice. Dissolve saffron and sugar in sauce. Cover and cook for 10 minutes. Let cool.

Note

Ratatouille tastes even better the next day. You can use it as a side dish, pasta sauce, filling for a quiche or an omelette, or over quinoa for a full vegetarian meal. It freezes beautifully so make a few batches in the summer before the tomatoes disappear.

Ingredients

1/3 cup olive oil

2 1/2 pounds onions, thickly sliced

1 1/2 pounds eggplant, cut into chunks (about 1/2x2 inches square)

1 1/2 pounds sweet peppers, seeded and sliced

1 pound zucchini (about 4 small), quartered lengthwise and cut into thirds

2 pounds sun-ripened tomatoes, coarsely chopped with their juice

5 to 6 sprigs fresh thyme

2 pinches saffron

1 sugar cube

Submitted by:
A Friend of WQED Pittsburgh

From the Garden

America's
HOME COOKING
Pasta

Bacon-Tomato Angel Hair

Directions

In a large skillet, cook bacon until crisp. Drain, reserving 1/4 cup drippings. Return drippings to skillet. Add bacon, green onion and garlic; cook for 1 minute. Stir in tomatoes, basil, salt and pepper. Simmer for 5 minutes. Prepare angel hair pasta according to package directions; drain. Add pasta to tomato mixture and toss to blend. Garnish as desired and serve immediately. Refrigerate leftovers. Serves 2.

Ingredients

6 slices bacon, cut up

2 tablespoons sliced green onion

1 clove garlic, minced

2 tomatoes, peeled and chopped

1/2 teaspoon basil leaves

1/2 teaspoon salt

1/8 teaspoon pepper

1/4 (1-pound) package angel hair pasta, uncooked

Submitted by:
Charlene Kula, Greensburg

Garden Gravy

DIRECTIONS

Place all ingredients except cream and pasta on a baking sheet and set under an oven's broiler. Once tomatoes are bubbling and everything is cooked through, move ingredients to a blender. Blend ingredients and add a bit of cream. Serve over pasta of your choice with some fresh asiago and parmigiano reggiano.

INGREDIENTS

2 pounds Roma tomatoes

2 small Spanish onions

1 small eggplant

1 zucchini

1 roasted red pepper

1 bunch basil

1 bunch parsley

Few leaves of oregano

3 to 4 large garlic cloves

Olive oil

Salt and pepper

Cream

Pasta, for serving

Asiago and parmigiano reggiano, for garnishing

America's
HOME COOKING

SUBMITTED BY:
Ernie Francestine

Handmade Cavatelli

Directions

Mix flour, egg, ricotta and salt. Gradually add more flour until a fairly stiff dough forms. Knead dough on a floured board until it is smooth and no longer sticky. Let rest for 5 minutes, covered with a bowl. Divide dough into 4 or 5 small balls and roll each ball into a thin rope (about 1/4 inch in diameter). Cut rope into 1/4-inch pellets and dust them lightly with flour. Using the inside of a cheese grater, roll each pellet against the grater with the tip of a finger. (This creates a macaroni shaped like a hollow football with a bumpy exterior from the grater's indentations.)

Lightly flour a large tray and place cavatelli in a single layer to dry slightly. After about 2 hours, bring 4 quarts of salted water to boil and drop in cavatelli a few at a time. Boil for approximately 6 minutes. Drain and serve with pesto or any sauce.

Note

It takes a little practice and a little patience to roll the cavatelli, but my Aunt Mary taught all of us to do this by the time we were 5 years old. I'm sure you'll get the hang of it—or find a five year old!

Submitted by:
Chris Fennimore, WQED Pittsburgh

Ingredients

1 cup flour

1 egg

1/2 cup ricotta

1/4 teaspoon salt

Marinara Sauce

DIRECTIONS

Heat sauté pan and add olive oil. Finely chop onion and sauté slowly until onion is translucent. Crush and mince garlic (a little salt will help to keep it on the cutting board). Cut tomatoes into 1/4-inch pieces. Add tomatoes and garlic to onions in pan. Bring heat up to moderate and cook until tomatoes break down slightly, about 10 minutes. Add freshly chopped basil, salt and pepper to taste.

Pour over 1/2 pound of a favorite pasta and serve.

INGREDIENTS

4 tablespoons olive oil

1 medium onion, finely chopped

1 clove garlic, crushed and minced

8 plum tomatoes

3 tablespoons fresh basil

Salt and pepper

1/2 pound cooked pasta, for serving

America's
HOME COOKING

SUBMITTED BY:
Chris Fennimore, WQED Pittsburgh

Spaghetti with Summer Herbs

DIRECTIONS

Prepare pasta in a large pot of salted water, until al dente, and drain. Place olive oil in a skillet and cook breadcrumbs over medium heat, stirring, until golden and crisp. Transfer to a bowl and set aside. In a large serving bowl, combine herbs, shallots or scallions, extra virgin olive oil and unsalted butter. Add drained spaghetti to herb mixture, tossing to coat evenly. Season pasta with pepper and sprinkle with breadcrumbs. Top with freshly grated parmesan cheese, if desired. Serves about 6.

INGREDIENTS

1 pound angel hair or other thin spaghetti

1 1/2 tablespoons olive oil

1 cup fresh breadcrumbs

2 cups chopped or shredded assorted summer herbs, such as parsley, basil, chives, thyme, tarragon, mint or other summer herbs of your choice

3 small shallots, finely chopped (3 scallions, white and green parts, finely chopped, can be used as a substitute)

4 tablespoons extra virgin olive oil

3 tablespoons unsalted butter, cut into bits

Freshly ground black pepper, to taste

Freshly grated parmesan cheese (optional)

SUBMITTED BY:
Debbie Chuba, Johnstown

89

Sweet Harmony

DIRECTIONS

Prepare a pan of water to cook pasta. When water boils, add a scant teaspoon salt. Preheat a sauté pan and then add olive oil, onions and garlic in order, cooking until translucent. Add parsley and oregano, cooking and stirring for 1 minute. Add wine and tomatoes, stirring until warm. Add a little salt and more black pepper. Finally, add imitation crab meat, cooking only until heated through. Drain pasta; put in pasta bowl and cover with sauce. Enjoy with a salad and white wine with a fruit dessert. Serves 6.

INGREDIENTS

1 pound long, thin pasta

2 tablespoons olive oil

1/2 sweet onion, diced

5 to 6 green onions, chopped

1 clove garlic, crushed, or
1/2 teaspoon minced garlic

2 tablespoons fresh parsley,
chopped, or 1 teaspoon
dried parsley

1 tablespoon fresh oregano,
chopped, or 1/2 teaspoon dried
oregano

1/3 cup dry white wine

6 big, ripe tomatoes, peeled and
diced, or 1 (28-ounce) can diced
tomatoes (if seeds are to be
removed, do so with a sieve to
keep tomato liquid)

Salt and freshly ground black
pepper, to taste

1 pound imitation crab
meat, thawed, chopped and
refrigerated

America's
HOME COOKING

SUBMITTED BY:
Jan Stivanson, Pittsburgh

Tomato-Zucchini Stir Fry

DIRECTIONS

Heat olive oil in a deep skillet; add diced zucchini, onion, hot peppers and garlic. Stir fry until zucchini is tender, about 5 minutes. Add tomatoes and basil; continue to cook for 3 minutes or until tomatoes are heated through. Serve over hot pasta. Serves 4.

INGREDIENTS

2 tablespoons olive oil

2 medium zucchini, diced

1 medium onion, sliced

2 hot peppers, sliced (optional)

1 clove garlic, pressed

4 large garden-ripe tomatoes, chopped

1 teaspoon basil

Salt and pepper, to taste

1 pound cooked pasta

SUBMITTED BY:
Diane Barnes, Fairmont

From the Garden

America's
HOME COOKING
Salads and Dressing

Broccoli-Tomato Salad

DIRECTIONS

In a large salad bowl, combine broccoli, cauliflower, bacon, onion, tomatoes and eggs; set aside. In another bowl, combine mayonnaise, sugar and vinegar; mix until smooth. Just before serving, pour dressing over salad and toss. Serves 6 to 8.

INGREDIENTS

1 bunch broccoli, separated into florets

1 head cauliflower, separated into florets

8 bacon strips, fried and crumbled

1/3 cup chopped onion

1 cup tomatoes, seeded and chopped

2 hard-cooked eggs, sliced

1 cup mayonnaise or salad dressing

1/3 cup sugar

2 tablespoons vinegar

SUBMITTED BY:

_ola Olinski, Maynard

Cucumber-Tomato Yogurt

DIRECTIONS

Cut cucumbers lengthwise into halves. Scoop out seeds and cut cucumbers into 1/2-inch pieces. Mix cucumbers, tomatoes, onions and parsley; cover and refrigerate. Mix yogurt, salt and cumin; cover and refrigerate. At serving time, drain vegetables and fold into yogurt dressing. Garnish with additional chopped cucumbers and tomatoes, if desired.

INGREDIENTS

2 medium cucumbers

2 medium tomatoes, chopped

2 green onions with tops, chopped

1 tablespoon snipped parsley

1 (8-ounce) carton unflavored yogurt

1/2 teaspoon salt

1/4 teaspoon ground cumin

America's
HOME COOKING

SUBMITTED BY:
Lola Olinski, Maynard

Fresh Tomato Salad

DIRECTIONS

Mix all ingredients. Italian or balsamic vinaigrette salad dressing can be substituted.

INGREDIENTS

3 to 4 tomatoes, cut into large pieces

1 cucumber, peeled and cubed

1 onion, thinly sliced

1 tablespoon balsamic vinegar

3 tablespoons olive oil

Salt and pepper, to taste

SUBMITTED BY:
Helen Skalski

Harvest Vegetable Salad

DIRECTIONS

Combine vegetables in a large bowl. Beat mustard, vinegar, garlic and wine together with a wire whisk. Add a few drops of oil at a time and whisk together. Season with salt and pepper. Add tarragon leaves to vegetables. Pour dressing over all and toss. Serves 24.

NOTE

You may add pasta to make a heartier salad. Just be sure to double the dressing to cover all of the salad.

INGREDIENTS

3 pounds carrots, julienned

3 pounds zucchini, cut into rounds

2 pounds fresh mushrooms, sliced

4 large sweet red peppers, cut into strips

5 cucumbers, sliced

4 pints cherry tomatoes, halved

24 radishes, sliced

1 large head cauliflower, cut into florets

DRESSING:

3 tablespoons Dijon mustard
1/2 cup red wine vinegar

3 cloves garlic, crushed

1/4 cup cabernet wine

1 cup olive oil

Salt and pepper, to taste

Fresh tarragon leaves

America's
HOME COOKING

SUBMITTED BY:
Susan Mihalo VanRiper, Allison Park

Italian Tomato, Mozzarella and Basil Salad

Directions

For marinade/dressing, combine vinegar, garlic, salt, dry mustard and pepper. Slowly add oil in a steady stream while whisking constantly. Whisk until well blended.

Slice tomatoes and mozzarella cheese 1/4 inch thick. Trim cheese until it is about the same size as sliced tomatoes. Place cheese and tomatoes into a shallow 13x9-inch glass dish and drizzle with marinade. Cover with plastic wrap and refrigerate for 1 to 3 hours. Turn tomatoes and cheese occasionally. Just before serving, stack basil leaves with largest leaf on the bottom. Roll up leaves and then slice into very thin strips. Arrange tomatoes and cheese slices on a nice platter, alternately. Sprinkle with slices of basil and drizzle with marinade.

Ingredients

2 tablespoons red wine vinegar

1 clove garlic, minced

1/2 teaspoon salt

1/4 teaspoon dry mustard

Freshly ground black pepper

1/3 cup olive oil or vegetable oil

4 large plum tomatoes

6 ounces mozzarella cheese

10 fresh basil leaves

Submitted by:
Carolyn Moschak, Pittsburgh

Lamb, Cucumber and Tomato Salad

DIRECTIONS

Combine lamb, cucumber, tomatoes and lettuce; toss lightly. Add remaining ingredients; toss lightly, but thoroughly.

INGREDIENTS

2 cups diced cooked lamb

1 medium-size cucumber, thinly sliced

2 medium-size tomatoes, diced

4 cups torn lettuce

1/2 cup dairy sour cream

Salt, to taste

Pepper, to taste

America's
HOME COOKING

SUBMITTED BY:
Charlene Kula, Greensburg

Make Ahead Salad

DIRECTIONS

In a flat-bottom casserole or salad bowl (about 9 inches across and 4 1/2 inches deep), layer ingredients (through parmesan cheese) in the order listed. Cover with plastic wrap until airtight. Refrigerate overnight or at least 8 hours.

Before serving, garnish with tomatoes or grape tomatoes, hard-cooked eggs and bacon. Makes 10 or more servings.

INGREDIENTS

1 large head of lettuce, broken into bite-size pieces

1 cup chopped celery

1 or 2 medium-size red onions, sliced into thin rings

1 (8-ounce) can water chestnuts, drained and sliced

1 (16-ounce) package frozen peas, separated and not cooked

2 cups mayonnaise (spread like frosting, approximately 1/2 inch thick)

2 teaspoons sugar

Grated parmesan cheese, about 1 cup

Tomatoes or grape tomatoes, quartered, for garnishing

Hard-cooked eggs, quartered, for garnishing

6 to 12 slices bacon, cooked and crumbled, for garnishing

SUBMITTED BY:
K. Darlene Wiggins, Pittsburgh

Pomegranate Carrot Salad

DIRECTIONS

Wash and grate carrots into a large bowl. Wash and grate apples and stir into carrots. Stir in lemon juice, canola oil, dried fruits and maple syrup. Stir in seeds from pomegranate and stir. Serves 8.

NOTE

This recipe is a slaw that keeps well for several days and gets sweeter. I prefer to use all organic ingredients. The organic carrots are sweet enough that some feel no additional sweetener is necessary.

This salad is juicy so serve with a slotted spoon. It is a great summer refresher. I use it as a snack instead of cookies, cakes, etc.

Whole pomegranates are available in autumn only. They keep well in the refrigerator. The seeds can be bought year round in the refrigerated section of some supermarkets.

INGREDIENTS

4 carrots, washed and grated to yield about 2 cups

4 crisp, dry apples (such as winesap), washed and grated to yield about 2 cups

1/4 cup lemon juice

1/3 cup canola oil

1 cup dried fruits (such as cranberries, apricots, blueberries and cherries)

1/3 cup maple syrup

1 pomegranate (seeds should yield at least 1/2 cup)

America's
HOME COOKING

SUBMITTED BY:
Sandra Gould Ford

Raw Cauliflower and Gorgonzola Cheese Salad

Directions

Cut away core of cauliflower heads. Break each apart into individual florets. Holding florets with stem pointing up, thinly slice each one. Put cauliflower into a large bowl and add cheese, parsley and basil.

Whisk together mustard and vinegar in a medium bowl. Whisk in olive oil a few drops at a time. Add garlic and season with salt and freshly ground pepper. Pour dressing over salad. (The dressing will taste strongly of vinegar. This will decrease during marinating.) Cover and chill for 1 hour before serving. Salad can be spooned onto individual lettuce leaves for individual portions or poured over broken up lettuce leaves to serve. Serves 12.

Note

This salad can be made the night before it's needed.

Ingredients

2 medium heads cauliflower

1/2 pound gorgonzola cheese, crumbled

1/2 cup chopped parsley leaves

1/4 cup chopped basil leaves

12 leaves romaine lettuce

Vinaigrette Dressing:

2 heaping tablespoons Dijon mustard

1/2 cup white wine vinegar

1 1/4 cup olive oil

1 clove garlic, crushed

Salt and freshly ground pepper, to taste

Submitted by:
Susan Mihalo VanRiper, Allison Park

Summertime Picnic Relish

DIRECTIONS

In large skillet, cook and stir onion and green pepper in oil over medium heat until tender. Stir in remaining ingredients; heat to boiling. Cool. Cover; refrigerate for several days.

Makes 3 cups.

NOTE

This recipe is good for sandwiches, hot dogs and hamburgers.

INGREDIENTS

1 cup finely chopped onion

1 cup finely chopped green pepper

2 tablespoons salad oil

3 cups peeled, chopped tomatoes

2 tablespoons vinegar

1 1/2 teaspoons salt

1/2 teaspoon sugar

1/4 teaspoon dry mustard

1/8 teaspoon pepper

America's
HOME COOKING

SUBMITTED BY:
Lola Olinski, Maynard

Tomato Toast Salad

DIRECTIONS

Mix dressing of olive oil, garlic, wine vinegar and basil. Marinate tomatoes in dressing for about 30 minutes. Toast French bread slices under broiler until golden brown. Arrange 3 toast slices on 2 plates; top with tomatoes, onions and bell pepper. Serves 2.

INGREDIENTS

3 tablespoons olive oil

1 clove garlic

2 tablespoons wine vinegar

1 teaspoon basil

6 Roma or plum tomatoes, diced

6 slices French bread, toasted

1 small red or sweet onion, thinly sliced

1 small bell pepper, thinly sliced

SUBMITTED BY:
Diane Barnes, Fairmont

Tomato Vinaigrette

Directions

Arrange tomato slices in an 8-inch square dish and set aside. In a small bowl, whisk together oil, vinegar, garlic, oregano, salt, pepper and mustard; pour over tomatoes. Cover and chill for 1 to 2 hours. To serve, place each lettuce leaf on an individual plate and top with 2 tomato slices. Drizzle with dressing; sprinkle with onions and parsley. Serves 6.

Ingredients

12 thick tomato slices

1/2 cup olive oil

2 to 3 tablespoons red wine vinegar

1 clove garlic, minced

1 teaspoon snipped fresh oregano

1/2 teaspoon salt

1/4 teaspoon pepper

1/4 teaspoon dry mustard

6 large lettuce leaves

Minced green onions, for garnishing

Minced fresh parsley, for garnishing

America's
HOME COOKING

Submitted by:
Julia Gyure, Daisytown

Tomatoes and Cucumbers in Sour Cream
(Pomidory i Ogorki with Smietanie)

DIRECTIONS

Combine tomatoes, cucumber and onion in a medium bowl. In a small bowl, combine sour cream, salt and pepper. Stir sour cream mixture into tomato mixture until vegetables are evenly coated. Cover and refrigerate until ready to serve. Serves 4 to 6.

NOTE

This recipe can also be made with salad dressing and sugar in place of sour cream and salt and pepper. Just sweeten salad dressing to taste and stir into tomato mixture.

INGREDIENTS

4 medium tomatoes, each cut into 8 wedges

1 medium cucumber, peeled and sliced

1 medium onion, chopped

1/2 cup sour cream

1/2 teaspoon salt

1/8 teaspoon ground white pepper

SUBMITTED BY:
Lola Olinski, Maynard

Tropical Mango Avocado Salad

DIRECTIONS

Prepare salad dressing according to directions on package using canola oil and apple cider vinegar. Shake to mix well.

Peel and chop mango into 1/4-inch cubes. Peel and chop avocado into 1/4-inch cubes. Combine mango, avocado, red onion and 1/2 of Italian dressing, stirring to combine well. Chill in refrigerator until ready to dress salad. Wash and tear romaine lettuce into bite-size pieces. Sprinkle with peeled and cut jicama. Serve with dressing on top.

INGREDIENTS

1 (1-ounce) envelope Italian salad dressing mix

Canola oil

Apple cider vinegar

1 ripe mango

1 ripe avocado

1/4 cup diced red onion

Romaine lettuce

1/2 cup jicama (cut into matchsticks)

America's
HOME COOKING

SUBMITTED BY:
Nancy Weinstein

From the Garden

America's
HOME COOKING
Soups and Stews

Celeriac Vichyssoise

Directions

Sweat onions in olive oil until soft, but not browned. Add garlic and cook for 1 minute. Add all chopped vegetables, parsley and bullion. Add water. Cover and cook until vegetables are soft. Use stick blender, blender or food processor and process until smooth. Add sour cream and blend until smooth. Serves 4. Soup can be served hot or cold.

Ingredients

1 large onion, chopped (about 1 cup)

1 teaspoon olive oil

1 clove garlic, minced, or 1/2 teaspoon garlic powder

1 large potato, peeled and chopped (about 1 cup)

1/2 large celeriac root, peeled and chopped

1/2 yellow squash or zucchini, chopped

1 cup celery (including leaves), chopped

2 tablespoons fresh parsley, chopped

2 packets chicken bullion

Water to cover vegetables, about 2 to 3 cups

1/2 cup fat-free sour cream

Submitted by:
Nancy Weinstein

Fall Clean-Up

DIRECTIONS

In large skillet, place 2 tablespoons butter, shortening or oil of your choice. Add onions and garlic. Cook over medium heat, stirring until transparent. Add peppers and squash. Cook until soft, and then add tomatoes. Finish cooking when slightly thickened. Serve over rice as a side for any meal.

NOTE

Large batches can be frozen for future meals.

INGREDIENTS

2 tablespoons butter or other shortening

2 large onions, sliced in strips

1 clove garlic, sliced in slivers

2 cups peppers, sliced in strips

4 cups zucchini or any summer squash, sliced

4 cups half-ripe tomatoes

Salt, to taste

America's
HOME COOKING

SUBMITTED BY:
Esther Weyand-Landis, Somerset

Fresh Tomato Soup

DIRECTIONS

In a large saucepan, cook onion in butter until tender. Stir in flour to form a smooth paste. Gradually add water, stirring constantly until thickened. Add tomatoes, parsley, salt, sugar, thyme, bay leaf and pepper; bring to a boil. Reduce heat; cover and simmer for 20 to 30 minutes or until tomatoes are tender. Remove bay leaf. Garnish with lemon, if desired. Serves 4.

INGREDIENTS

1/2 cup chopped onion

1/4 cup butter or margarine

1/4 cup all-purpose flour

2 cups water

6 medium tomatoes, peeled and diced

1 tablespoon minced fresh parsley

1 1/2 teaspoons salt

1 teaspoon sugar

1 teaspoon minced fresh thyme or 1/2 teaspoon dried thyme

1 bay leaf

1/4 teaspoon pepper

Thin lemon slices (optional)

SUBMITTED BY:
Lola Olinski, Maynard

Gazpacho II

DIRECTIONS

Combine all ingredients except condiments and let sit for 1 hour. Puree in processor or blender and chill. Garnish with condiments. Serves 6.

INGREDIENTS

3 pieces French bread

6 very ripe tomatoes, peeled and copped

1 cucumber, chopped

1/2 cup chopped Bermuda onion

3 tablespoons olive oil

2 cups water

2 cups vegetable broth

2 cloves garlic, peeled

2 tablespoons wine vinegar

1 teaspoon cumin

1 tablespoon sweet basil

2 teaspoons salt

CONDIMENTS:

1 green pepper, minced

1 cucumber, minced

Croutons

Hard-cooked egg, minced

1 avocado, cubed

America's
HOME COOKING

SUBMITTED BY:
Susan Mihalo VanRiper, Allison Park

Greens, Potato and Sausage Soup

DIRECTIONS

Place cooking oil in a large pot, add sausage and brown on medium heat, about 10 minutes. Remove sausage to cool; slice and reserve. Add onion and garlic to pot (add oil if needed) and cook for 5 minutes on low heat.

Add broth, water, salt and pepper and bring to a boil. Add sliced sausage and diced potatoes and bring to a simmer. Add greens a handful at a time, stirring to wilt. Simmer, covered for 15 minutes, until potatoes and greens are tender.

INGREDIENTS

1 teaspoon cooking oil

1 pound chicken or turkey sausage

1 small onion, chopped

4 cloves garlic, minced

1 quart low-sodium chicken stock

2 cups water

1 teaspoon salt

1/4 teaspoon pepper

2 pounds potatoes, diced

1 pound kale or collard, stems removed and chopped

1/2 teaspoon red pepper flakes, or to taste

SUBMITTED BY:
Teri Shaw, Valencia

115

Mom's Seven Up

DIRECTIONS

Preheat oven to 350 degrees. Cook and crumble bacon. Combine all other ingredients and bring to boil on stove. Add crumbled bacon (bacon grease maybe added for more flavor). Transfer to baking dish. Top with biscuits. Place in oven until biscuits are brown.

INGREDIENTS

8 slices bacon, cooked and crumbled, reserving grease

4 cups fresh corn, green beans and carrots, and frozen peas

1 medium onion, chopped

1 small head cabbage, chopped

1 quart canned tomatoes

1 green pepper

1 cup water

Salt and pepper, to taste.

Biscuits, using either baking mix or canned biscuits, for serving

America's
HOME COOKING

SUBMITTED BY:
Skeet's and Lynne Shawley, North Huntingdon

Old-Fashioned Tomato Soup

DIRECTIONS

Cook tomatoes until soft; add a pinch of salt. When soft, add soda. Heat milk and butter until butter is melted. Add tomatoes to milk slowly. Add salt, pepper and celery salt, to taste. (Don't let mixture boil.) Serve with toasted bread or crackers.

INGREDIENTS

1 pint ripe, peeled tomatoes

1/8 teaspoon baking soda

1 quart milk

1 tablespoon butter

Salt, pepper and celery salt, to taste

Toasted bread or crackers, for serving

SUBMITTED BY:
Allegra Farsht, Jennerstown

Poached Garden Eggs

DIRECTIONS

Roughly chop veggies in fairly large pieces. Sauté everything except tomatoes in olive oil in large skillet until soft. Add a generous amount of quartered fresh tomatoes (skins on or off, overripe tomatoes work great) and continue cooking over medium to low heat for about 15 minutes. Bring skillet up to a nice simmer and add cracked, whole eggs right into skillet to poach in the vegetable/tomato sauce. Allow at least 1 or 2 eggs per person. Spoon sauce over eggs, cover and cook until eggs are done to your preference. Bring the whole skillet to the table and serve family style with lots of good bread to sop up all the juices.

NOTE

My mom would make this often in the summer when the garden was producing. It was quick, inexpensive and didn't heat up the kitchen. We never sat down at the table for any meal without a loaf of good bread (homemade or Mancini's), but this meal always required a minimum of 2 loaves.

INGREDIENTS

Miscellaneous vegetables from the garden such as onions, eggplant, zucchini, garlic and tomatoes

Olive oil

Salt and pepper, to taste

Eggs

America's
HOME COOKING

SUBMITTED BY:
Marisa Tobias, Sewickley

Polish Tomato Soup
(Zupa Pomidorowa)

DIRECTIONS

Melt butter or margarine in a large skillet. Add tomatoes; cover and cook over medium heat for about 20 minutes or until skins shrivel, stirring occasionally. Pour tomatoes into a fine-mesh strainer. With a wooden spoon, press tomatoes through strainer into a large bowl, mashing pulp and liquid through strainer. Discard tomato skins and seeds.

Place broth or bouillon in a large sauce pan. Bring to a boil over medium heat. Add strained tomatoes or tomato paste. In a small bowl, combine flour and sour cream. Stir 1 cup tomato mixture into flour mixture, then return mixture to sauce pan. Stir into tomato mixture until smooth. Add sugar. Season with salt, to taste. Simmer over low heat for 5 minutes. Serve hot. Garnish with parsley or dill. Serves 8 to 10.

INGREDIENTS

3 tablespoons butter or margarine

4 pounds ripe tomatoes, quartered (about 16 medium tomatoes) or 1 (6-ounce) can tomato paste

2 quarts chicken or meat broth or bouillon

3 tablespoons all-purpose flour

1 cup sour cream

1 tablespoon sugar

Salt

Chopped fresh parsley or dill, for garnishing

SUBMITTED BY:
Lola Olinski, Maynard

Sassy Potato Corn Chowder

Directions

Cook bacon in large saucepan until crisp. Drain and return to pan. Stir in potatoes, broth, corn, onion and celery. Bring to a boil. Reduce heat to low. Simmer 15 minutes or until potatoes are tender. Mix flour and dressing. Stir in milk, and then add to potato mixture. Continue cooking for 3 to 5 minutes or until thoroughly heated. Sprinkle with additional bacon and parsley, if desired.

Ingredients

4 slices bacon, chopped

3 cups cubed, peeled potatoes (about 1 1/4 pounds)

1 (13 1/2-ounce) can chicken broth

2 cups fresh corn, cut from cob

1/2 cup chopped onion

1/2 cup chopped celery

2 tablespoons flour

1/2 cup salad dressing

2 cups milk

Parsley, for garnishing

America's
HOME COOKING

Submitted by:
Lola Olinski, Maynard

Slew

DIRECTIONS

In a medium pot, heat oil and butter. Sauté onion until transparent. Add tomatoes and cook 5 to 10 minutes allowing tomatoes to soften and release juices. Add remaining vegetables and season to taste. Add enough water to allow mixture to steam. Cover pot and cook on low heat about 30 minutes or until vegetables are tender. Slew can be served over a bed of rice. Serves 4.

INGREDIENTS

2 tablespoons olive oil

2 tablespoons butter

1 medium onion, diced

1 quart tomatoes (about 6 to 8 medium tomatoes), peeled, seeded and cut into chunks

1 medium zucchini, sliced

2 to 3 potatoes, sliced

1 green pepper, diced

2 cups string beans

1 cup water

Salt and pepper, to taste

SUBMITTED BY:
Pauline Cleaver, Revloc

Spring Root Stew

DIRECTIONS

Place ham cut side down in bottom of a slow cooker. Top with everything except potatoes. Add water to cover. About 2 hours before end of cooking, add potatoes. (If you add them too soon, they will be mush.) Cook for a total of 6 hours at least. Remove vegetables. Take out ham and pick off the meat and add to bowl of vegetables. Serve with a side of applesauce and biscuits.

INGREDIENTS

The end of a ham, about 4 to 5 inches thick

6 large parsnips, chunked

6 large turnips, chunked

6 large carrots, sliced in rounds

6 stalks celery, sliced in 1-inch pieces

2 large onions, cut into a large dice

2 cloves garlic, sliced in slivers

1 teaspoon coarse black pepper

1/2 teaspoon nutmeg

2 tablespoons Worcestershire sauce

6 large potatoes, chunked

Applesauce, for serving

Biscuits, for serving

America's
HOME COOKING

SUBMITTED BY:
Esther Weyand-Landis, Somerset

Strawberry Soup with Pound Cake Croutons

DIRECTIONS

Place strawberries and orange juice in a blender or food processor and puree. Strain mixture into a 4-quart saucepan. Mix tapioca with 1/4 cup strawberry mixture. Add to saucepan along with spices. Heat to boiling, stirring constantly. Cook for 1 minute. Pour soup into a blender and add sugar, lemon peel, lemon juice and buttermilk. Blend until smooth (or add all ingredients and use an electric whisk). Chill at least 2 hours.

Preheat oven to 325 degrees. Spread pound cake cubes in a single layer on a cookie sheet. Bake for 6 to 19 minutes or until lightly browned.

Divide soup into bowls and top with a few croutons. You also can garnish with a thin sliver of lemon and strawberry. Serves 4.

INGREDIENTS

2 pints fresh strawberries

1 cup fresh orange juice with no pulp

1 1/4 tablespoons instant tapioca

1/8 teaspoon allspice

1/8 teaspoon cinnamon

1/2 cup sugar

1 1/4 teaspoons grated fresh lemon peel

1 tablespoon fresh lemon juice

1 cup buttermilk

1 1/2 cups pound cake (cut into 1/2-inch cubes)

SUBMITTED BY:
Jim Baran, O'Hara Township

From the Garden

America's
HOME COOKING
Canning and Preserving

24-Hour Zucchini Pickles

DIRECTIONS

Heat vinegar, sugar and spices in a saucepan. When sugar is dissolved and mixture has come to a boil, turn off heat and add zucchini, onions and salt. Refrigerate for up to a month.

INGREDIENTS

3/4 cup vinegar

3/4 cup sugar

1/4 teaspoon mustard seed

1/4 teaspoon celery seed

1/4 teaspoon turmeric

3 cups sliced zucchini

1 cup sliced onion

Dash salt

SUBMITTED BY:
Audrey Casperson, White Oak

Gourmet Bar-B-Q Sauce

DIRECTIONS

Peel, seed and finely chop peaches and pears or put through a food mill or puree in food processor. Add to prepared tomatoes and put in heavy kettle or Dutch oven. Remove bay leaves and turmeric seeds from pickling spice jar and tie remaining spices in a cheese cloth bag. Add to kettle with remaining ingredients and stir well. Simmer, stirring occasionally, for 1 to 2 hours until it reaches proper consistency. Remove bag of spices while sauce is still hot and pour into 1/2 pint or pint jars or freezer containers. Process or freeze.

NOTE

This sauce smells and tastes great and is perfect for barbecue on the grill or added to browned hamburger for sloppy joes or chipped ham for barbecue sandwiches.

INGREDIENTS

3 large ripe peaches

3 large ripe pears

15 to 20 large ripe tomatoes, peeled, seeded and cut into a medium dice

1 (1 3/4-ounce) box or jar mixed pickling spice

3 medium onions, finely chopped

1 cup finely chopped celery

2 cups sugar

2 cups cider vinegar

1 teaspoon salt

America's
HOME COOKING

SUBMITTED BY:
Carolynne L. Lewis, Ford City

Grandma's Green Tomato Mincement

DIRECTIONS

Take 6 heaping cups chopped or shredded tomatoes and cover with water. Add 1/2 cup salt and let stand overnight. (Don't use a metal container.) Drain in a sieve and run cold water over tomatoes to rinse off most of salt. Press out as much liquid as possible. Don't skip or shorten this step—it takes the bitterness out of tomatoes. Place tomatoes in a very large pot and add apples, raisins, brown sugar, cider vinegar and spices. Bring to a full boil and then reduce heat and simmer until thick, about 2 to 3 hours. Add butter (not margarine or other spreads) and rum or rum extract. Seal in hot jars. A quart jar will make an 8- or 9-inch pie and a pint will make a batch of cookies or tarts. Use straight from the jar or add applesauce to make it less rich.

INGREDIENTS

6 heaping cups finely chopped or shredded tomatoes

1/2 cup salt

6 cups grated tart apples

3 cups raisins

4 cups brown sugar

1 1/3 cups cider vinegar

1 tablespoon cinnamon

1 teaspoon cloves

3/4 teaspoon each allspice, mace and black pepper

2 teaspoons salt

3/4 cup butter

1 cup rum or 1/2 bottle rum extract

SUBMITTED BY:
Deborah McCanna, East Brady

Green Tomato Relish

DIRECTIONS

In a large saucepan, add enough water to cover tomatoes, peppers, onions and vinegar. Cook over medium heat. After 30 minutes, add remaining spices and cook for another 30 minutes. Feed mixture through a meat grinder. This relish is delicious for meats and sandwiches.

INGREDIENTS

18 tomatoes (3 small tomatoes equals 1 large)

4 red peppers

2 green peppers

6 onions

4 cups cider vinegar

1 teaspoon cloves

3 teaspoons salt

1 teaspoon cinnamon

1 teaspoon allspice

10 tablespoons white sugar

America's
HOME COOKING

SUBMITTED BY:
Evelyn Goodhart, Pittsburgh

Peperoni All'Agrodolce
(Sweet and Sour Pickled Peppers)

DIRECTIONS

Bring salt, sugar, oil and vinegar to boil; turn off burner and put pepper strips in liquid to marinate overnight. They must stay in liquid for at least 24 hours; proceed with canning.

Take a clean jar and layer peppers and combined spices, filling jar to top. Leave enough space to fill with marinade and let sit overnight. Follow canning/pickling procedure, and boil jars for at least 10 minutes in water. Store in a cool, dry area.

INGREDIENTS

1/2 cup salt

2 cups sugar

1 1/2 cups vegetable oil

1 liter wine vinegar

10 to 12 pounds red, green and yellow peppers, cut into strips

Chopped parsley, minced garlic and bay leaves

SUBMITTED BY:
Phyllis Loffredo Mancinelli

Piccalilli

Directions

Slice tomatoes and leeks. Cover with salt and water. Let stand overnight. Drain salt water, and then put tomatoes and leeks in a large pot. Add sugar, vinegar and pickling spice. Boil for 10 to 15 minutes and then jar. These are delicious on any sandwich or use instead of relish or garnish.

Ingredients

20 to 30 green tomatoes

10 leeks

3/4 cup salt

1 1/2 cups water

4 1/2 cups sugar

2 1/2 cups apple vinegar

1 (1 3/4-ounce) jar pickling spic

America's
HOME COOKING

Submitted by:
Dolly Venezia, Pittsburgh

Pomodori Secchi
(Grilled Dried Tomatoes)

DIRECTIONS

Wash, dry and halve tomatoes. Either sun-dry or slow grill them until completely dried out. Put vinegar in a bowl and once tomatoes are dried rinse them in vinegar and then squeeze dry. Proceed with canning.

Place a layer of tomatoes, some spices and continue to layer to top. Leave enough room to fill the top with olive or vegetable oil. Do not close jars immediately—wait until the next day. An extra day will allow the oil to work its way down to bottom and the jar may need more in order to preserve tomatoes. Store jars in a cool, dry area.

INGREDIENTS

2 to 3 pounds ripe Roma tomatoes

2 cups wine vinegar

Red pepper flakes, oil and salt, to taste

Basil, garlic, capers and mint, to taste

SUBMITTED BY:
Phyllis Loffreda Mancinelli

Spicy Quick Dill Pickles

DIRECTIONS

Wash pint jars well. In the screw-top jar, mix together salt, sugar and vinegar until sugar is dissolved.

Into each jar, place 4 garlic halves, dill sprigs, 2 hot peppers and cucumber quarters. Pour 1/4 of brine over pickles. Add about 1/12 teaspoons coriander seeds to each jar. Top off jars with enough water to cover pickles. Close jars and refrigerate for 24 hours or up to 1 month.

NOTE

Hot peppers are optional. You can leave them out. Happy pickling!

INGREDIENTS

3 tablespoons kosher salt

2 tablespoons sugar

1 1/4 cups white vinegar

8 cloves garlic, sliced in half

Fresh dill sprigs

8 hot chilies (optional)

6 pickling cucumbers or 3 regular cucumbers, washed well, cut into quarters (to fit pint jars)

2 tablespoons coriander seeds

America's
HOME COOKING

SUBMITTED BY:
Barbara Knezovich, McKeesport

Tomato Butter

DIRECTIONS

Combine all ingredients and cook together slowly for 3 hours, stirring frequently. Store in glasses as you would jelly. Seal air tight.

INGREDIENTS

5 pounds ripe tomatoes

2 pounds sugar

1 or 2 cups mashed apples

Cinnamon stick

Ginger, mace and cloves, to taste

Juice and rind of 1 lemon

1/4 cup vinegar

SUBMITTED BY:
Helen Fullerton, Pittsburgh

Tomato Jelly

DIRECTIONS

Combine tomatoes and sugar. Stir until sugar is dissolved. Bring to a boil and cook for 15 minutes. Remove from heat and add gelatin directly from the package. Mix well. Pour into sterile jars. Seal and refrigerate.

INGREDIENTS

5 cups peeled and seeded tomatoes

3 3/4 cups sugar

1 (6-ounce) package strawberr' gelatin

America's
HOME COOKING

SUBMITTED BY:
Honey Kolsun, Pittsburgh

Zucchini Stew

DIRECTIONS

Sauté onion and pepper in butter until browned. Add tomatoes and zucchini. Cook until almost tender. Braise hamburger and drain. Add it to stew and continue cooking until tender. Add salt and pepper. Serve with a chunk of homemade Italian bread.

NOTE

I make this in large quantities and can it. I cook mine until zucchini pieces lose their white color. (I do not add meat until I open the jars.) I put zucchini into jars and add 1 teaspoon or less salt to each quart and seal jars. Process it in a water bath for 2 hours. When I open a jar, I add meat and then simmer for 20 to 30 minutes.

INGREDIENTS

1 onion, diced

1 green pepper, diced

1 piece hot pepper, diced (optional)

Butter or margarine

1 quart tomatoes (canned or fresh)

1 quart diced, peeled and seeded zucchini

1 pound ground hamburger (or sliced wieners)

Salt and pepper, to taste

SUBMITTED BY:
Hazel Wiles, Smithfield

From the Garden

America's
HOME COOKING
Dessert

Butternut Squash Bake

DIRECTIONS

Preheat oven to 350 degrees. In a mixing bowl, cream butter and sugar. Beat in eggs, milk and vanilla. Add squash and blend well. (It will seem curdled.) Pour into a 11x7-inch pan. Bake uncovered for 45 minutes or until almost set.

Combine topping ingredients and sprinkle over casserole. Return to oven for 5 to 10 minutes or until bubbly. Let set for a few minutes before cutting into squares to serve. Serves 6 to 8.

INGREDIENTS

1/3 cup butter, softened

3/4 cup sugar

2 eggs

1 (5-ounce) can evaporated milk

1 teaspoon vanilla extract

2 cups mashed cooked butternut squash

TOPPING:

1 cup crisped rice cereal

1/4 cup packed brown sugar

1/4 cup chopped pecans

2 tablespoons butter, melted

SUBMITTED BY:
Dorothy Rezzolla, Indiana

Butternut Squash Brown Sugar Pie

DIRECTIONS

To make crust, preheat oven to 375 degrees. Combine ground cookies with sugar and butter in a food processor and pulse 8 times or until combined. Press mixture into a 9-inch pie plate. Bake for 6 minutes. Cool.

Put squash and water in a microwave-safe bowl and cook until very tender. Drain well and mash squash. Combine squash with remaining ingredients in a medium saucepan. Cook over medium heat until thick, about 8 minutes, stirring constantly. Pour mixture into baked crust. Bake at 375 degrees for 20 minutes or until set. Cool. Pie may be served with whipped cream.

INGREDIENTS

CRUST:

1 cup finely ground gingersnap (approximately 22 cookies)

1 tablespoon sugar

1 tablespoon butter, melted

FILLING:

3 cups peeled and cubed butternut squash

3 tablespoons water

3/4 cup evaporated fat-free milk

2/3 cup packed brown sugar

1 1/2 teaspoons cinnamon

3/4 teaspoon ground ginger

1/4 teaspoon salt

1/4 teaspoon nutmeg

1/8 teaspoon cloves

2 large eggs

America's
HOME COOKING

SUBMITTED BY:
Annemarie O'Toole, South Fayette

Chocolate Zucchini Cake

DIRECTIONS

Preheat oven to 325 degrees. Cream margarine, oil and sugar. Add eggs, vanilla and sour milk. Beat with mixer. Mix together dry ingredients and add to creamed mixture. Beat well with mixer. Stir in zucchini. Spoon batter into a greased and floured 9x12-inch pan. Sprinkle top with chocolate chips. Bake for 40 or 45 minutes until toothpick inserted near the center comes out clean.

INGREDIENTS

1/2 cup margarine, softened

1/2 cup vegetable oil

1 3/4 cups sugar

2 whole eggs

1 teaspoon vanilla

1/2 cup sour milk

2 1/2 cups flour

4 tablespoons cocoa

1/2 teaspoon baking soda

1/2 teaspoon cloves

2 cups finely diced zucchini

1/4 cup chocolate chips

SUBMITTED BY:
Regina Rosky, Jeannette

143

Fresh Strawberry Glazed Pie

DIRECTIONS

Place washed fresh strawberries in pie shell. Bring cornstarch, sugar and water to a boil in a saucepan. Stir until thick and clear. Remove from heat and quickly stir in gelatin. Pour warm mixture over strawberries in pie shell. Refrigerate until cool—at least 1 hour or overnight. Enjoy with a dollop of whipped cream/topping.

INGREDIENTS

3 cups whole or sliced strawberries

1 (9-inch) pre-made graham cracker pie crust

3 tablespoons cornstarch

1 1/2 cups water

3/4 cup sugar

1 (3-ounce) box strawberry gelatin

America's
HOME COOKING

SUBMITTED BY:
Hilary Zubritzky, McKees Rocks

Mock Apple Pie

Directions

In a large pot, combine zucchini and lemon juice; add enough water to cover. Cook until tender.

Combine crumb ingredients together.

Preheat oven to 375 degrees. Add sugar, cinnamon and 1/2 cup of crumb mixture to pot. Simmer about 1 minute. Pat 1/2 of remaining crumb mixture into a 13x9-inch pan. Bake for 10 minutes. Add zucchini and remaining crumb mixture and bake 15 minutes longer or until brown.

Ingredients

8 cups peeled and diced zucchini with seeds removed

2/3 cup lemon juice

1 cup sugar

1 teaspoon cinnamon

Crumb Mixture:

4 cups flour

1 1/2 cups (3 sticks) margarine

1/2 teaspoon salt

2 cups sugar

Pineapple-Rhubarb Pie

Directions

Preheat oven to 350 degrees. Mix first 6 ingredients and cook on stove top over medium-low heat until thick. Pour mixture into unbaked pie crust. Mix first 4 topping ingredients and cut in butter. Pour on top of pie. Bake for 30 minutes. If pie starts to run over, turn oven down to 275 degrees. Cool on baking rack.

Ingredients

PIE:

2 cups rhubarb

2 cups canned crushed pineapple, drained

3/4 cup sugar

2 tablespoons cornstarch

2 eggs beaten

1/2 teaspoon salt

1 unbaked pie crust

TOPPING:

1 cup oatmeal

1/2 cup brown sugar

3 tablespoons flour

1/2 teaspoon

2 tablespoons butter

SUBMITTED BY:
Tracy Schrock, Holistic Health Counselor

Spiced Berry Compote

Directions

Heat honey, lemon juice and spices in a large skillet until mixture begins to simmer. Remove skillet from heat. Add berries and gently toss to coat with honey mixture. Place in a large bowl and cool to room temperature. Divide berries among serving bowls. Drizzle with yogurt and garnish with mint leaves and lemon zest.

Ingredients

1/2 cup honey

2 teaspoons fresh lemon juice

1/8 teaspoon each cinnamon, allspice, nutmeg, ginger, cloves, anise and cardamom

2 pints assorted fresh berries (strawberries, blueberries, raspberries, blackberries)

1/4 cup nonfat lemon yogurt

Fresh mint, chopped, for garnishing

Grated fresh lemon zest, for garnishing

SUBMITTED BY:

Jim Baran, O'Hara Township

Index

24-Hour Zucchini PIckles 127

A

Asparagus and Red Pepper
Sauté 55

*Asparagus with Lemon Garlic
Aioli. 9

B

Bacon-Tomato Angel Hair. 85

Baked Green Tomatoes 21

Baked Whole Tomatoes 22

Breaded Tomatoes with Cheese
Sauce 23

Broccoli Stir Fry 56

Broccoli-Tomato Salad 95

Bruchetti 24

Butternut Squash Bake 141

Butternut Squash Brown Sugar
Pie 142

C

Carolyn's Country Garden Quiche 25

Celeriac Vichyssoise 111

Chocolate Zucchini Cake 143

Corn and Basil Egg Roulade 57

*Corn and Red Pepper Fritters. 10

Corn and Rock Shrimp Pot Pie 58

Cornmeal Biscuit Dough. 59

*Creamy Basil Roasted Garlic Tomato
Soup. 11

Crepes 75

Crunchy Fried Tomatoes 26

Cucumber-Tomato Yogurt. 96

E

Easy Pan Fried Tomatoes 27

Eggplant Pizza 76

Eggplant Pudding. 77

F

Fall Clean-Up 112

Fesenjan-e Bademjan 78

Fire and Ice Tomatoes 28

Fresh Strawberry Glazed Pie. 144

Fresh Tomato Salad 97

Fresh Tomato Soup 113

Fried Green Tomatoes 29

G

Garden Gravy. 86

*Recipes were prepared on "America's Home Cooking:
From the Garden"

Index

*Garden Tomato Tart 12

Gazpacho I 60

Gazpacho II 114

Glazed Carrots 61

Gourmet Bar-B-Q Sauce 128

Grandma's Green Tomato
Mincemeat 129

Green Tomato Relish 130

Greens, Potato and Sausage
Soup 115

Grilled Zucchini with Feta 43

H

Handmade Cavatelli 87

Haricots Verts in Walnut Oil 62

Harvest Vegetable Salad 98

I

Italian Tomato, Mozzarella and Basil
Salad 99

J

Jan's Good Tomato Recipe 30

L

Lamb, Cucumber and Tomato
Salad 100

M

Make Ahead Salad 101

Marinara Sauce 88

Mediterranean Fish with Fennel and
Kalamata Olives 63

Mediterranean Tomato Salad 31

Mixed Vegetables 64

Mock Apple Pie 145

Mock Crab Cakes 44

Mom's Seven Up 116

O

Old-Fashioned Tomato Soup 117

Old Stone Inn Corn Fritters 65

P

Peperoni All'Agrodolce 131

*Pesto 13

Pesto Chicken 66

Piccalilli 132

Pineapple-Rhubarb Pie 146

Plum Tomato Tart 32

Poached Garden Eggs 118

Polish Tomato Soup 119

*Recipes were prepared on "America's Home Cooking:
From the Garden"*

Index

Pomegranate Carrot Salad. 102

Pomodori Secchi 133

R

*Raspberry Balsamic Vinaigrette 14

Ratatouille. 79

Ratatouille Crepes 80

Raw Cauliflower and Gorgonzola
Cheese Salad. 103

*Rhubarb Oatmeal Crisp Dessert. 15

Roasted Ratatouille 67

S

Salsa. 33

Sassy Potato Corn Chowder 120

Scalloped Tomatoes. 34

Skillet Vegetables. 68

Slew 121

Spaghetti with Summer Herbs 89

*Spectacular Butternut Squash
Ravioli 16

Spiced Berry Compote. 147

Spicy Quick Dill Pickles 134

Spring Root Stew 122

Stewed Tomatoes. 35

Strawberry Soup with Pound Cake
Croutons. 123

Stuffed Fried Cubanella Sweet
Peppers 69

Stuffed Zucchini Boats 45

Succotash. 70

Summer Ratatouille 81

Summertime Picnic Relish 104

Sweet Harmony 90

Swiss Chard, Beans and
Tomatoes 71

T

Tomato and Cheese Strata 36

Tomato Butter. 135

Tomato Fans. 37

Tomato Jelly 136

Tomato Pie 38

Tomato Toast Salad 105

Tomato Vinaigrette 106

Tomato-Zucchini Stir Fry 91

Tomatoes and Cucumbers in Sour
Cream. 107

*Recipes were prepared on "America's Home Cooking:
From the Garden"

Index

Tomatoes Oregonata 39

Tropical Mango Avocado Salad. . . . 108

Y

Yellow Tomato Coulis 40

Z

*Zucchini Casserole 17

Zucchini Cheesecake 46

Zucchini Flowers with Goat Cheese and
Mint. 47

Zucchini Fritters 48

Zucchini Pancakes 49

Zucchini Parmesan. 50

Zucchini Quiche 51

Zucchini Stew. 137

Zucchini Stuffing Casserole 52

America's HOME COOKING

*Recipes were prepared on "America's Home Cooking:
From the Garden"*